POCHA

POCHA

SU SCOTT

Simple Korean Food from the Streets of Seoul

Hardie Grant

QUADRILLE

To my father,
Seoul will always be
our forever home.

The Beating Heart + Soul of Seoul

Pocha; short for *pojangmacha*, which literally translates as 'covered wagon'; pocha is a tented or tarpaulin-covered stall, bar or market vendor serving up cheap and unfussy Korean comfort food, snacks and drinks.

I remember so fondly the very first time I took my daughter to Gawngjang Market in Seoul. She was almost two years old and still in her buggy. We were having to carefully navigate the narrow and crowded alleyways with an excitable child who could not sit still. Her little legs swung merrily from her seat as she squealed, and she frequently jumped in amazement at the hustle and bustle that was entirely new and yet not so strange at all.

It was almost November in Seoul. The autumn was waning, with a noticeable chill clutching our skin at night. Under the sheltered halls of the tarpaulin-roofed market, the air was cold, but the rising steam in the distance looked cosy and welcoming, with an occasional gust of wind carrying the waft of something delicious. Dust motes glittered in the glow of orange tungsten lights, moving quickly through the streams of neon light travelling with the traffic.

It felt warm there. People sat closely together, shuffling their bums along to accommodate another stranger, a couple or small group of tourists on the bench. The seats were snapped up just as quickly as food appeared on the makeshift tabletops of various food stalls. Plates clinked and glasses were cheered to the rhythm of honking motorbikes in the distance. Market traders touted for business over the jumble of music from the shops nearby. Every corner of the market echoed with happy chatter, the living and breathing sound of this fast-moving city weaving in and out to create an electric atmosphere and magical ambience.

We followed the hot steam, enticed by the warm air that carried such appetizing smells. People queued up for cheesy corn dogs filled with salty ham and mozzarella. There were golden nuggets of fried chicken piled high, with drizzles of rich caramel-like soy sauce that dripped lusciously onto the craggy crusts. The oil was so hot you could feel the heat radiating from the cauldron. I could smell the sugar and spice. The sound of deep-frying was infectiously inviting and made me salivate instantly.

We strolled the market as though it was our playground, completely immersed in the vibrant colours of the city I grew up in. My child tasted the same fish-shaped pastry filled with sweet red bean paste that I used to love eating when the cold evenings painted the streets steely blue. She drank the same milk I grew up with, straight from the carton, and my heart swelled with joy that I was able to share this small piece of my home.

Six long years later, I returned to Seoul with my family. After all the years of absence, the air felt foreign but everything smelled familiar. We walked the streets, old and new, eating our way through the crowded corners of Seoul to feel its beating heart and soul. We ate sticky brown sugar-stuffed hot pancakes for a little pick-me-up when the 4pm slump hit our jet-lagged bodies hard and fast, and slurped late-night pot noodles from the convenience store as we perched at the kerbside tables for fun. My now seven-and-a-half-year-old daughter knew all the lyrics of the K-pop songs playing in the street and fell in love with the crazy, fast vibe of a city full of 24/7 street snacks and cute stationery.

I carry so many tender food memories shaped around the streets and markets I frequented over the years. The pungent smell of fermented pickles takes me back to the small alleys of the local market where my mother shopped for her groceries. We snacked on freshly fried fishcakes and ate steamed dumplings or pork buns to fill our bellies cheaply and cheerfully. My maternal grandmother ran an old-school fried-chicken shop in a market on the outskirts of Seoul where no frills and no menu served people a good eat that was homely and comforting. My youth was filled with the smell of *tteokbokki*, which instantly brings me sweet memories of after-school hangouts with friends, chatting innocently about pop stars and teenage pimples and short skirts and heartaches that used to make us feel like the world was ending.

Slowly rotating fans and mosquito strips hanging precariously from the roof of pocha in summer bring me the happiness of balmy evenings. I remember cooling August showers that made my feet squelch, but a bowl of plain and simple udon noodles slurped under the rain was always perfectly cosy and tasty. What is offered in the streets of Seoul isn't anything fancy. But the plates nurse our hunger with comfort, and the flavours soothe our soul. People's stories are layered thickly onto the sticky tabletops; the rich history of the city is etched deeply into the cooks' hands, which glow radiantly with kindness and generosity; our feelings grace the streets with laughter and tears.

Every time I wander through Seoul, my heart races with a feeling of being truly alive. And I feel deeply privileged to be able to share the culture of Korean street food, which continues to withstand the constant changes of a city that seems to grow and expand globally at the speed of light. In Seoul, days move fast and nights stay young and free. Tradition and modernism co-exist symbiotically, and while foreign influence is welcomed and embraced to broaden our vision and experience, the preservation of traditions has always held great importance.

Perhaps you will find joy in the reminiscent taste of something familiar, or these recipes sprinkled generously with new and exciting flavours will make you feel inspired to rush to the kitchen. Either way, I hope the collection of snacks and dishes gathered here give you a taste of Korean hospitality that is warm and generous. Please pull up a chair. Gather a few friends, if you like. And enjoy the spirit of the city that is never without deliciousness, 24/7.

Su x

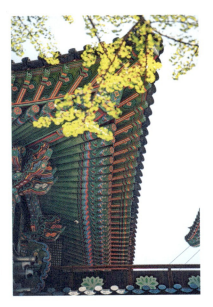

A Brief History
of Pojangmacha

Pojangmacha – or pocha, the short name we usually use – literally means
a small, tarpaulin-covered cart, selling modest snacks and street food. The
term pocha has grown beyond this literal translation to convey a part of Korean
food culture, and there are many theories behind its origins. Some believe it
originated from Japanese food carts that operated on Korean roadsides during
the Japanese occupation of the early 20th century. Others suggest it is rooted
in the ancient tradition of Korean pedlars selling small goods and food. However,
the most likely origin of what we now recognize as *pojangmacha* are the simple
handcarts of the 1950s, shielded by a thick cotton cloth, that could be seen
on so many streets, serving noodles, soju by the glass and simple snacks such
as grilled sparrow (which remained common until the 1960s).

Coinciding with the establishment of tarpaulin production in Korea in
the 1960s and the economic growth period of the 1970s, the popularity of
pojangmacha grew steadily and these modest spots on the street became places
to rest, welcoming industrious city workers with their friendly atmosphere and
generous hospitality.

Pocha was – and still is – the place where people gather to offload the
weight of a laborious life from their shoulders; a therapeutic environment
where each person can tell their story and be comforted and listened to, with
food as the medium to share experiences and to build a human connection
that sustains and supports our daily existence.

In the 1980s, pocha entered a boom period. The country's continuing
economic growth meant more people had disposable income and could afford
to dine out more. Once considered as a place only for the working class, people
from all walks of life gathered at pocha for a casual evening out with friends
to share some cheap and cheerful food offerings, known as anju, and a few
rounds of soju.

Sadly, during the mid 1980s – around the time when Seoul hosted the Asian Games and the Olympics – the government, keen to portray a positive image of Seoul to the increasing number of foreign visitors, started to tightly control the growth of pocha with stricter legislation in an effort to build a smarter and cleaner city. While the modern restaurant businesses began to thrive and expand rapidly around that time, many *pojangmacha* spots across Seoul disappeared and their future became uncertain.

During the economic downfall in 1997, demonstrating the truly resilient spirit of the nation, *pojangmacha* started to rise once again, this time in the form of indoor restaurants that retained a street-food vibe. People recently out of jobs invested their retirement or redundancy payouts into pocha with a vision for a fresh start as they required little upfront money to set up. Many former city workers became owners or chef owners of nostalgic drinking establishments, promising affordably priced food and drinks for customers. This creative adaptation of taking what was once a makeshift set-up with a few plastic tables and bar stools into an indoor space equipped with more comfortable seats and proper toilets started to gain popularity and established itself as a genre of its own: indoor pocha.

Nowadays, only very few allocated outdoor *pojangmacha* spots remain across Seoul, namely in Jongno or Euljiro, and in and around some of the city's old traditional markets. If you are lucky, you might come across one of the bright red-orange tarp-covered stalls selling nostalgic plates of my all-time favourite dishes, cooked simply and deliciously, peppered with a humour and grit that makes you feel good. While some may feel the quality isn't as good as it used to be and everything is overpriced and small portioned, the point of these places is that they are how Seoul learned to nurse the hunger of the people. They are the very fabric of Seoul that fed the aspiring nation's soul – enabling the country to flourish into the ultra-modern powerhouse it is now. For that, I hope, this somewhat fading tradition finds its way to continue its rich culture and legacy. Pocha is the Seoul I would like to preserve.

Bringing the Pocha Vibes Home

Pocha, by its nature, is casual and relaxed, so however you are using this book
– whether it is to gather friends together to host a pocha party at home or for
a quiet solo meal – just remember it is all about having a good time without any
fuss. All you need is a place to eat, be it at a table with chairs or sitting on a comfy
sofa with your plate on your lap, and maybe with some candles or lights twinkling
in the background. Whatever makes your life easier is a go.

Pocha food is homely and rustic but skilfully crafted with simple cooking
and convenience in mind, and almost always enjoyed with an alcoholic drink.
Most of the recipes in this book are straightforward and quick and easy to prepare;
the few exceptions are slow cooked, so the oven does most of the work. While
traditional flavours are cherished and highly sought after, modern flavours from
near and far have been welcomed in Korea and deeply penetrate both professional
and domestic kitchens, broadening the ranges of cuisines available within
the country. You can detect the measured influence of travels both inwards
(in the form of an increasing number of foreign visitors) and outwards.

The most popular drink served at pocha is soju, which can be found in Korean
supermarkets or online. It is a clear, colourless distilled alcoholic beverage made
from rice and grains that is consumed cold and neat in a small shot glass. While
more common varieties offer an average AVB of 17 per cent or below, some of the
finest hand-crafted soju can contain anything between 25 per cent to near 50 per
cent alcohol. Soju is typically unflavoured and has a clean taste not dissimilar to
vodka, although many brands continue to develop fruit-flavoured soju with a lower
alcohol content, as well as developing premium-grade soju with on-point labels
that have a wider appeal to the modern crowd. Some of the modern iterations are
often crafted with different ageing techniques and tasting profiles. They can taste
quite different from what most people recognize as soju – I've tried some that
tasted like tequila! These stronger types are designed to be sipped slowly with

or without ice, or to combine with mixers to dilute the alcohol and to bring out the flavour. See the chapter (page 230) dedicated to a small selection of soju-inspired cocktails to get you started.

The other common drinks offered in pocha are lager-style beers or *makgeolli*, which is a popular traditional Korean rice wine that is lower in alcohol, averaging below 10 per cent. It is made from a simple concoction of steamed rice, yeast and water. Once combined, the rice mixture is left to ferment for a few weeks to develop its unique chalky colour and subtle effervescence. The bubbles tend to be small, and the drink feels slightly denser than water and silkier on the tongue. It tastes subtly sweet and mildly tangy with a bitter undertone that pairs well with a broad range of food. In recent years, interest in *makgeolli* has grown – in much the same way soju has evolved – with younger generations looking into better ways to preserve the tradition and culture. Cleverly marketed micro-brewery types have started to pop up across small and unassuming corners of Korea, offering an aesthetically pleasing environment to enjoy the traditional wine and modern food parings.

An Accessible Modern Korean Pantry

At the time of writing this book, we are in the midst of a cost-of-living crisis that focuses our awareness on the challenges we face to balance our income and outgoings. I felt it was an appropriate time to review the consumer choices I am making, being mindful not only of the cost of ingredients and energy but being considerate of the sources of energy, accessibility of products, transport and environmental impact.

The recipes in the book use what is mostly commonly found in our kitchens; there's nothing exclusive or overly expensive. I simply encourage you to buy the best fresh produce you can afford and handle them with care to get the most out of them. Cooking with in-season ingredients and buying local produce will help to keep the cost down, as you will be eating what is in abundance and therefore much more cost-effective. I frequently reach out for canned or frozen produce and I have tried to put an emphasis on both affordability and convenience because I truly believe good food should be accessible to all.

Essential Storecupboard Basics

A well-stocked, hard-working pantry can take a basic, mundane ingredient and elevate it to create a dish packed with exciting flavours. I have tried to create simple combinations and recipes requiring few ingredients and little time and energy, to deliver the flavours that satisfy. I believe simple cooking stems from confidence in ingredients and process and we should not feel bad or embarrassed about adopting a few shortcuts. Most staple ingredients used repeatedly throughout this book are hopefully already commonly used in your kitchen, especially if you are already familiar with Korean or other East and South East Asian cooking. If you'd like to learn more about Korean flavours and ingredients, you'll find detailed information and an extensive list of common Korean pantry items in my first book, *Rice Table*.

Flavourings

The main Korean flavours are often built around the trio of *jang*:

- *doenjang* (fermented bean paste)
- *gochujang* (fermented chilli paste)
- *ganjang* (soy sauce)
+ the cheerful red flakes of *gochugaru* (Korean red pepper flakes).

These are the cornerstones of Korean cuisine that build the uniquely pungent savoury depth of flavour. I use multipurpose Japanese soy sauce as my standard soy sauce with the addition of light or soup soy sauce, fish sauce, oyster sauce, shrimp paste, *yondu* (seasoning sauce), Worcestershire sauce and sea salt flakes to season and layer different kinds of salinity and umami.

Golden granulated sugar is most commonly used in my cooking with occasional use of caster (superfine), soft brown, Demerara or icing (confectioners') sugar. Mirin (sweet rice wine), honey, *jocheong* (rice syrup) and blackstrap molasses (treacle) are also used to add sweetness.

Rice vinegar, cider vinegar and some seasonal citrus fruits are frequently used for acidity.

Grains + Noodles

The rice used throughout is white short-grain rice often labelled as sushi rice, with the exception of Kimchi Risotto (page 51). Most of the recipes will work with brown short-grain rice too if that is what you prefer; just soak the grains in water to hydrate fully (preferably the night before or at least for a few hours), to soften the grains before cooking as per the instructions.

Korean instant noodles appear here and there, which are both delicious and convenient. Thin dried wheat noodles and Korean sweet potato noodles are great storecupboard basics. And I recommend stocking up on frozen udon noodles as they are superbly toothsome and cook in no time.

Dasima + Gim or Gim jaban

Dasima is dried kelp, also known by its Japanese name *kombu*, which I use to make quick stocks to add subtly sweet and delicate ocean-like saltiness.

Gim or *gim jaban* is a dried seaweed that can be found either as a large sheet or crumbled. The former can come both seasoned and unseasoned but the latter is always toasted and seasoned. It is a real powerhouse storecupboard ingredient that can add salty-sweet umami flavour. Use it liberally as desired. Nori sheets are the same but are typically unseasoned.

Oils

I use cold-pressed rapeseed (canola) oil or sunflower oil for general cooking that requires high heat – listed as vegetable oil throughout the book. Extra virgin olive oil also appears frequently as I use it regularly in my kitchen. Korean toasted sesame oil is superbly fragrant, as is perilla oil, which has beautiful cumin-seed-like aroma and anise taste.

Practical Kitchen Ideas

I wrote this book in a tiny shoe-box-sized kitchen in between moves with a broken ring on the stove and a small sink that didn't even fit an oven tray. You can safely assume that the recipes gathered here are completely do-able in any kitchen of any capacity. You don't need fancy gadgets or tools; all you need is enthusiasm and a few basic kitchen essentials such as a sharp knife and decent pots and pans.

Mise en Place

Happy cooking requires an organized set-up where everything is laid out clearly in front of you to follow through the recipe. This French culinary term meaning 'putting in place' or 'gather' really is your best friend. Read through the recipe. Prepare the ingredients as guided so you are well set from the get go.

Have a waste bowl to collect peels and unwanted scraps – some peels and scraps can be stored in a resealable bag in the freezer until you have enough to make delicious stock, with or without the addition of meat bones and carcass.

Portion + Freeze

Some of the recipes, especially the slow-cooking ones, offer up to 6 servings. Instead of reducing the recipe, cook the entire batch to maximize energy use and simply divide the portion into freezer-safe containers for later use. Most of the recipes keep well in the freezer.

Swap the Proteins + Vegetables

Korean home cooking is all about being intuitive and adaptable, so feel free to adapt the recipes with other similar ingredients available in season in your locality. All I ask is that you cook the recipe once as written so you can learn from your own experience what might make a good substitute.

Seasoning + Heat Level

I like my food seasoned savoury – a good balance of full flavour. Acidity is used frequently to add a brightness to the dish, while bitterness brings a welcome layer of umami that we often overlook. Sugar used in non-sweet recipes brings out the savouriness in the same way salt is often used in sweet recipes to accentuate the sweetness. I have a fairly tolerant heat (as in chilli hot) threshold, so the level of spiciness here can be quite bold for those with lesser tolerance. But I do hope that the flavours are pleasantly balanced to taste and that you enjoy the dishes.

Equipment

Mandoline: A fair bit of preparation requires julienning vegetables. Investing in a decent mandoline and knowing how to use it safely can save some time. Or practise your knife skills to make the prep a breeze.

Thermometer: While I believe in intuitive cooking that involves a more sensory approach of relying on the nose, hands and eyes, sometimes, especially when you feel less certain about the type of cooking, having a reliable measure can be incredibly useful to achieve the results you want. A decent digital thermometer can be a great tool for checking when meat is ready, for example, or ensuring the correct temperature for deep-frying in a pan.

Rice cooker: If you have a space for it, having a rice cooker really makes a huge difference.

Timings

While the utmost care has been taken to ensure the accuracy of the timings and therefore the best results, there are other influencing factors – such as the size of the pan you're using, the power of your heat source, effectiveness of heat retention of the pan, the moisture content of raw ingredients – which can all affect the cooking time. I hope the recipes are guided with plenty of cues to confidently lead you, so use your senses as well as the timer.

Miscellaneous

Garlic and ginger throughout the recipes are peeled unless otherwise stated, and minced or grated using a knife, fine grater, pestle and mortar or a garlic crusher. Two teaspoons of ginger is about 10g (¼oz).

For mild chilli varieties I use serrano, or jalapeños for green chillies, and the long Spanish type for the red; for hotter varieties, I use bird's eye or finger chillies.

Onions used in the recipes are mostly brown Spanish onions, and all vegetables are peeled and cleaned unless otherwise stated.

Eggs are always free-range in mixed weights; where size of the egg is important, the weight is specified.

Happy cooking!

For Breakfast, Lunch or Dinner · Bunsik

ALL DAY DINING

For Breakfast, Lunch or Dinner

Here is a selection of fast flavours from convenience stores and early-morning street vendors.

Silky Egg Porridge

Gyeran Juk

Tender grains of rice swollen plump and soft, rice porridge is often the thing I associate with nourishment and comfort. All the better made with two staple ingredients: rice and egg. I like the restrained simplicity that allows me to truly appreciate the faint sweetness of humble everyday rice and the silky strands of velvety egg that add volume and sustenance to a dish that can otherwise be a little thin.

SERVES 4

160g (5¾oz/scant 1 cup)
    short-grain white rice
1 tbsp perilla oil
1.1 litres (37fl oz/4½ cups)
    water
1 tbsp *yondu*
    (seasoning sauce)
1 heaped tsp light
    or soup soy sauce
1 tsp ground white pepper
2 eggs, lightly whisked
    with a pinch of salt
sea salt flakes, to taste
a pinch of sugar (optional)

To finish

1 spring onion (scallion),
    thinly sliced
a little thinly julienned
    root ginger
gim jaban (crumbled toasted
    seasoned seaweed)
a few drops of chilli
    oil (optional)

Place the rice in a large bowl and rinse thoroughly by swishing it or rubbing it between your hands until the water runs almost clear. Drain, then fill the bowl with cold water and let the rice soak for at least 30 minutes. When ready, drain the rice using a fine sieve and set aside.

Gently heat the perilla oil in a heavy-based saucepan with a lid over a low–medium heat. Add the drained rice and sauté for a minute to coat in the oil, stirring occasionally to stop the grains from sticking to the pan. You will notice the fragrant aromas of perilla oil and in a minute or two, the grains of rice will start to appear translucent, at which point they will also start to stick to the pan more.

Gradually add the water, stirring to incorporate the rice into the liquid with control. Stir in the *yondu*.

Cover with the lid, increase the heat and bring the mixture to a high simmer. Reduce the heat to low and simmer gently for 25 minutes with the lid on ajar. Stir every now and then to ensure the rice does not get stuck to the bottom of the pan. You should notice very gentle bubbles erupting on the top and the blip-blip sound similar to the sound of simmering tomato sauce.

After 25 minutes, the rice should have broken down into a soft, creamy mush and the porridge thickened perfectly to a dropping consistency, when it falls off the spoon with a satisfying plop. Stir in the soy sauce and white pepper.

Carefully pour in the whisked eggs in a circular motion on top of the cooked rice, without stirring the pan. Leave to stand for 1 minute over a low heat. Remove from the heat and give it a gentle stir to incorporate the eggs into the rice. Check for seasoning and add salt to taste; sometimes a pinch of sugar can be added to taste, too.

To serve, divide between four individual bowls. Top each bowl with the spring onion, ginger and *gim jaban*. Drizzle with a little chilli oil, if liked, and serve warm.

Pine Nut Porridge with Oatmeal

Jat Juk

Convenience is in my mind when I think of this pine nut porridge. Typically made with a combination of blended rice and pine nuts, I actually rather used to like the taste of the instant packet version, which boasted a simple instruction to dissolve in water and cook for 4 minutes. It had a creamy and nutty taste with a pleasantly grainy texture that I really enjoyed. I am opting for porridge oats to create a similar kind of nostalgic magic in the wonder of 10 short minutes.

SERVES 2

50g (2oz/⅓ cup) pine nuts
90g (3¼oz/scant 1 cup)
   rolled porridge oats
400ml (13fl oz/1½ cups) water
100ml (3½fl oz/scant ½ cup)
   full-fat milk
sea salt flakes, to taste
clear honey, to taste
½ tsp toasted black sesame
   seeds, lightly crushed
   using a pestle and mortar

Place the pine nuts in a heavy-based saucepan and dry roast over a medium heat for 1–2 minutes to release the flavour. Leave them to cool, then tip into a food processor or spice grinder (reserving some for the garnish later) with half of the porridge oats and blend until fairly smooth.

Put the blended pine nut and porridge oat mixture and the rest of the oats back into the saucepan over a high heat. Add the water and milk to the pan and stir to combine.

Bring the mixture to just below the simmering point, then simmer gently over a low heat until it has turned soft and creamy, and the porridge has thickened perfectly to the consistency of thick custard; this will take about 7 minutes. Stir every now and then to ensure the porridge doesn't stick to the bottom of the pan. You should notice very gentle bubbles erupting while it cooks. Remove from the heat and season to taste with salt.

To serve, divide the porridge into individual bowls and drizzle with some honey to taste; it will help to balance the flavour and to bring out the savouriness. Top with the black sesame seeds and eat while warm.

Red Bean Porridge

Pat Juk

Traditionally, red bean porridge is a dish enjoyed on the day of the winter solstice. According to Korean folklore, red is the colour feared by ghosts, and many believe eating *pat juk* will ward off bad luck. The process begins with a long and slow simmer of red beans. The cooked beans are then blended with cooking water to separate the pulp and liquid; only the top liquid is used to produce the final porridge, mixed with a combination of pre-soaked glutinous rice or short-grain rice. A small portion of the pulp collected is stirred through towards the end of cooking to prevent the porridge from sticking to the pan. The whole process requires time, patience and above all, a lot of love.

I am taking a shortcut here by using canned aduki beans. While it may not be quite the same as the original, a gentle and careful simmer of rice and beans does reward you with a welcomingly warm bowl seasoned delicately with a slightly sweet edge.

SERVES 2–4

100g (3½oz/heaped ½ cup) short-grain white rice
400g (14oz) can of aduki beans
600ml (20fl oz/2½ cups) water
1 tbsp clear honey
sea salt flakes, to taste
a few finely chopped pine nuts, to garnish (optional)

Place the rice in a large bowl and wash thoroughly by swishing it or rubbing it between your hands until the water runs almost clear. Drain, then fill the bowl with cold water and let the rice soak for at least 30 minutes. When ready, drain the rice using a fine sieve and set aside.

Put a fine sieve over a heavy-based, lidded saucepan, tip the can of beans into the sieve and let the liquid drain into the pan. Put the beans aside. Add the pre-soaked rice along with 400ml (13fl oz/1½ cups) of the water to the pan. Bring just to the boil, cover with the lid, then simmer very gently for 15 minutes over a low heat, stirring every now and then to ensure the rice doesn't stick to the bottom of the pan.

Meanwhile, reserve one-third of the aduki beans; these will be added to the porridge at a later stage. Transfer the remaining two-thirds of the aduki beans to a blender, top with the remaining 200ml (7fl oz/scant 1 cup) of water, and purée until smooth.

After 15 minutes, add the puréed aduki beans to the rice pan, along with the reserved whole aduki beans. Give it a good stir and continue to simmer gently for a further 20 minutes over a low heat with the lid on ajar. Stir frequently. You should notice very gentle bubbles erupting through. The rice should have broken down into soft, creamy mush and the whole aduki beans should have softened perfectly but just about hold their shape. The porridge should have thickened to the consistency of runny custard.

Stir in the honey and season with flaky salt – for me this is about 1 heaped teaspoon. Add a touch more honey, if preferred. It should taste savoury with subtle sweetness. Divide into individual bowls and top with some pine nuts, if using. Serve while warm.

Bacon + Garlic Fried Rice

Bacon Maneul Bokkeumbap

SERVES 2

6 garlic cloves
2 tbsp vegetable oil
1 spring onion
   (scallion), sliced
4 rashers (slices) of
   smoked streaky bacon,
   sliced into small strips
300g (10½oz/1½ cups)
   cooked short-grain
   white rice (cold or warm
   but not steaming hot)
½ tsp sea salt flakes,
   or to taste
½ tsp ground white pepper
1 tsp toasted white sesame
   seeds, lightly crushed

Bitterness is a frequently overlooked flavour profile, but balanced with a touch of sweet, it can really amplify savoury dishes and create subtle notes of umami.

Don't be alarmed or put off by the amount of garlic here. The strong taste of garlic mellows as you fry; it becomes deliciously fragrant and embellishes the dish with a pleasantly bitter edge. Crispy garlic carries a sticks-to-your-teeth kind of gummy sweetness and contrasts with the tender grains of rice and salty bacon so perfectly. It's simply divine.

Prepare the garlic by lightly crushing and chopping three cloves and thinly slicing the rest. Have a plate lined with kitchen paper ready.

Heat the oil in a wok or frying pan (skillet) over a medium heat. Add the sliced garlic and fry for 2 minutes until lightly golden and crispy; you don't want it dark brown as it will become unpleasantly bitter. Transfer to the plate lined with kitchen paper and set aside until needed. Keep the oil in the pan for the next step.

Reduce the heat to low and stir in the chopped garlic and spring onion to gently warm up in the oil to infuse the flavours. Once the pan starts to sizzle and smells very fragrant, increase the heat to medium and add the bacon. Fry for about 3 minutes until the bacon turns crispy and the fat has rendered out.

Stir in the rice and season with the salt and white pepper. Continue stir-frying for 3 minutes, making sure you separate the grains of rice and toss all the ingredients together. Once the rice is piping hot, check for seasoning and adjust it with a pinch more salt, if needed. Remove the pan from the heat and divide between two bowls. Top with the reserved fried garlic and the sesame seeds and serve warm.

Bulgogi Rice Ball

Bulgogi Jumeokbap

Jumeokbap – which translates literally as 'fist rice' – is a seasoned rice ball shaped by hand. Often made using the odds and ends of ingredients you have to hand, its frugal nature and portability make it a great lunch-box filler or convenient snack. While some trace the origin of the dish to the Korean War in the early 1950s, one compelling story caught my eye during my research. Between the 18th and 27th May 1980, a democratic uprising took place in the southern city of Gwangju. The government pushed back hard and isolated the city in an attempt to control the movement. Street vendors from the city's traditional market – the majority of whom were female – came out onto the streets with pots of rice, hurriedly seasoned with only salt, and made *jumeokbap* to feed the hungry civilians fighting for democracy, who were mainly local students. Not surprisingly, for many locals, the dish remains a symbol of compassion, bravery and solidarity.

SERVES 2

150g (5oz) minced (ground) beef
scant 1 tsp vegetable oil
300g (10½oz/1½ cups) freshly cooked short-grain white rice
2 tsp toasted white sesame seeds, lightly crushed
1 tsp sea salt flakes
2 tbsp *gim jaban* (crumbled toasted seasoned seaweed)

For the beef marinade
1 garlic clove, minced
1 spring onion (scallion), minced
1 tbsp soy sauce
1 tbsp mirin
2 tsp golden granulated sugar
2 tsp toasted sesame oil
¼ tsp freshly cracked black pepper

Place the minced beef in a small mixing bowl along with all the marinade ingredients and combine well.

Heat the oil in a frying pan (skillet) or wok over a medium heat. Add the beef and the marinade and fry for about 5 minutes until the mince is browned and caramelized, stirring energetically to break up any big lumps and to stop the sugar burning. Cook the beef until there's no sauce left in the pan. Once done, remove from the heat and set aside until cool.

Place the warm, freshly cooked rice into a large mixing bowl. Add the sesame seeds, salt, *gim jaban* and the beef mixture. Using a rice paddle or spatula, stir to combine thoroughly without mushing the rice; folding from the edges to the middle of the bowl is a good way to keep things moving evenly. The rice should be cooled down enough to handle comfortably with bare hands. Check for seasoning and add a pinch more salt, if necessary.

Wearing a pair of latex gloves will help prevent the rice from sticking. If you are working with bare hands, wet your hands with water. Have a plate ready on which to place the shaped rice balls.

To shape, scoop some rice onto the palm of your dominant hand and shape the rice into a ball, using a cupping motion and your non-dominant hand to help shape, pressing firmly to form a tight ball. I like to make them about the size of a golf ball but you can make them whatever size you like, from bite-sized to literally a fist-sized ball. Continue shaping until you have used all the rice. Serve while warm.

Kimchi Risotto

Kimchi Juk

I came across various kimchi rice porridge pots and pouches in 24/7 convenience stores and supermarkets in Korea, which immediately reminded me of silky Italian risotto. The combination of kimchi and rice in a risotto was, for me, a completely obvious crossover between two cuisines I love.

Creamy Italian rice is seasoned with plenty of parmesan and kimchi; the tanginess of kimchi is softened with butter to mingle gently among the flavours that are familiar yet a little different, to pleasantly surprise the palate. Traditionalists on both continents may say this isn't either Korean or Italian but I would say it is a joyful union of both.

This is a recipe of two parts – the first stage is enjoying this kimchi risotto. The recipe makes enough for two for a cosy night in on a Friday evening, plus leftovers. You then use the leftovers to make Kimchi Arancini Scotch Eggs (page 52) some time during the weekend while you leisurely potter around the kitchen.

SERVES 2 + ENOUGH LEFTOVERS TO MAKE KIMCHI ARANCINI SCOTCH EGG (PAGE 52), OR SERVES 4 GENEROUSLY AS ONE MEAL

3 tbsp extra virgin olive oil
1½ onions, finely diced
sea salt flakes, to taste
300g (10½oz) kimchi, chopped
60g (2oz) unsalted butter
300g (10½oz/1⅓ cups) risotto rice
180ml (6fl oz/¾ cup) dry white wine (optional)
1 litre (34fl oz/4 cups) light chicken or vegetable stock, kept warm
1½ tbsp *doenjang* (Korean fermented bean paste)
100g (3½oz) parmesan, grated
freshly cracked black pepper, to taste
3 tbsp snipped chives
30g (1oz) *gim jaban* (crumbled toasted seasoned seaweed), optional

Heat the olive oil in a heavy-based saucepan over a low heat. Add the onions and a good pinch of salt. Sauté very gently for 10 minutes, stirring frequently, until evenly softened. You will notice fragrant aromas of the onion as it cooks down to release its natural sweetness. Stir in the kimchi and continue sautéing for about 8 minutes to gently caramelize everything together; you may want to increase the heat a touch towards the end if the kimchi still appears too wet.

Keep the heat to low–medium and add 20g (¾oz) of the butter to the pan, along with the rice. Stir energetically to evenly coat the rice in the melted butter and sauté for a couple of minutes until the grains of rice appear almost translucent in places. Add the wine, if using, and let it bubble rapidly for 1–2 minutes so that the alcohol evaporates and the liquid is absorbed into the rice.

Gradually add the warm stock a ladleful at a time, waiting for the rice to absorb the stock before adding any more, and stirring continuously. Stir in the *doenjang*. You may or may not need all the stock but gauge as you go along. Cook gently until the rice is cooked through but still with a little bite; it should take 15–20 minutes from the moment you stirred in the rice. You should notice the very gentle bubbles erupting through the grains of rice as you cook.

When the rice is cooked, remove from the heat and stir in the parmesan and the remaining butter. Beat vigorously together to incorporate the butter and cheese; the rice should be creamy and floppy enough to fall off the spoon easily. Add a touch more stock or water if it needs loosening a bit. Check the seasoning and adjust it with a pinch more salt and some black pepper to taste. Stir in the chives. Cover the pan and leave to rest for a couple of minutes to relax the grains.

Serve about two 350g (12oz) portions of risotto in two bowls and finish with a touch more parmesan, if you like. Serve while warm.

Stir the *gim jaban*, if using, into the remaining 750g (1lb 10oz) of risotto and transfer to a large flat tray or surface, spreading thinly to cool quickly. Once cooled, transfer to a lidded container and keep refrigerated for up to two days to make Kimchi Arancini Scotch Eggs overleaf.

Kimchi Arancini Scotch Eggs

Bansuk Kimchi Jumeokbap

The inspiration for this comes from the spicy seasoned rice balls sold in the convenience stores, which reveal a soft-set boiled egg in the middle. The fudgy egg in the cross-section initially reminded me of a Scotch egg, but then it led me onto thinking about arancini. So here is the second part of that Kimchi Risotto (page 51).

Is it arancini or is it a Scotch egg? Is it Korean? Does it matter? I don't think so! Because it is all those things fused together to form the flavours that represent everything I love about food, which is that we share more things in common than not. Deliciously seasoned carbs, studded with a soft sunshine-golden egg and deep-fried – what's not to like?

I like to serve this with a Japanese Worcestershire-style sauce such as okonomiyaki sauce.

MAKES 12 WITH QUAIL EGGS

12 quails' eggs
2 tbsp plain (all-purpose) flour, for dusting
1 egg, lightly whisked
60g (2oz/heaped 1 cup) panko breadcrumbs
750g (1lb 10oz) cooled Kimchi Risotto (page 51)
vegetable oil, for frying

Bring a pan of water to the boil – just enough to cover the eggs. Carefully lower in the eggs. Stir gently, put on the lid and simmer for 2½ minutes to give soft-boiled eggs. Lift the eggs out of the pan with a slotted spoon and submerge in a bowl of cold water to chill rapidly. When cool enough to handle, drain and tap the eggs gently against the surface to crack the shells a little, then peel very carefully.

Have four shallow, rimmed plates or trays ready: one to transfer the rice balls to as you go along, one filled with the flour, one with the lightly whisked egg and one with the panko breadcrumbs. Spray the breadcrumbs with a little water to moisten. Place a sheet of clingfilm (plastic wrap) on the work surface.

Spread about 60g (2oz) of risotto thinly in the middle of the clingfilm and wide enough to cover the egg. Roll one egg in the flour to coat lightly and place it in the middle of the rice. Start lifting up the corners of the clingfilm to help you cover the egg in the risotto, pressing gently but firmly to secure the rice onto the egg. This might feel a little fiddly but you will soon get the hang of it. Transfer to the plate or tray, then continue until you have used all the eggs and risotto. Once done, refrigerate for 20 minutes to firm up.

Keep one hand for the egg and the other for handling the dry ingredients. Lightly dust the rice balls with flour, dip into the whisked egg, then roll in the breadcrumbs gently but firmly until evenly coated. Transfer to a plate and repeat with the rest of rice balls.

Prepare a cooling rack set over a roasting tray so that you can swiftly transfer the cooked rice balls as you go along.

Fill a large, heavy-based saucepan or large frying pan (skillet) suitable for deep-frying with vegetable oil deep enough to submerge the balls but come no more than three-quarters of the way up the pan. Heat the oil to 170°C (340°F). Carefully lower a few of the rice balls into the oil, making sure you don't overcrowd the pan. Fry for 5 minutes until golden brown, crisp and cooked through, then transfer to a cooling rack while you fry the remaining balls. Serve while warm.

**USING
HENS' EGGS**

You could make four
larger eggs, if you like, using
hens' eggs (simmer for
5 minutes) and around
185g (6½oz) of risotto
for each egg.

Cheese + Pickle French Toast

French Toast

My first ever butter-fried toast sprinkled in sugar was cooked for me by my auntie; it was kind of a rarity in Korea back in the 1980s. The experience was so sensational! I can still remember the smell of butter and taste the cinnamon-dusted sugar. Little did I know back then that it was a riff on eggy bread. Fast forward a few decades, Western-influenced bakery goods are seen widely across Korea, from the tiny convenience store shelves to fancy dessert cafés with a strong practice of infusing both the traditional and non-traditional Korean baking techniques with European techniques. It's smart, impressive and actually really exciting.

The idea of sandwiching the cheese and pickle came about when I saw ham and cheese stuffed French toast sold in one of the convenience stores in Seoul, which I later learned is called a Monte Cristo. I like how the sharp and sweet chutney cuts through the richness of the eggy bread and complements the overall flavour. Enjoy it with a good drizzle of maple syrup and a splash of Tabasco.

MAKES 4 SMALL SQUARES

2 thick slices of white bread
1 tsp mayonnaise
1 tbsp small-chunk pickle (I use Branston)
2 slices of Port Salut or 1 slice of American cheese
a little unsalted butter, for frying

For the eggy mixture
1 egg
2 tbsp full-fat milk
1 tsp icing (confectioners') sugar
a pinch of sea salt flakes, to taste

To finish
maple syrup, to taste
a splash of Tabasco, to taste

Lay the slices of bread on a chopping board and spread the mayonnaise on one slice of bread and the pickle on the other. Put the cheese on top of the mayonnaise-smeared bread and cover with the other slice, with the pickle side facing inwards. Now you have the cheese and pickle sandwich. Cut into quarters so you have 4 small squares.

Make the eggy mixture by whisking all the ingredients in a shallow-rimmed dish snug enough hold the sandwich comfortably but without too much space. Carefully dip the cheese and pickle sandwich squares in the eggy mixture, turning on all sides to coat them evenly with the mix. Let the squares sit in the mix for 10 minutes to saturate fully, flipping over halfway.

Melt a small knob of butter in a non-stick frying pan (skillet) over a low heat. Place the egg-soaked sandwich squares in the pan and cook gently for 2–3 minutes on all sides until beautifully caramelized and golden in colour. You may want to melt in a little more butter from time to time.

Once done, transfer to a plate. The cheese should be beautifully gooey in the middle with specks of dark brown pickles within. Serve while warm with a drizzle of maple syrup and a few drops of Tabasco.

Korean
Street Toast

Gilgeori Toast

Korean street toast begins with a big chunk of butter in a vendor's well-gloved and skilful hand. The golden pool of omelette mixture, full of shredded white cabbage embellished with speckles of bright orange carrots and green spring onions, hits the pan in one big ladleful. It is pulled and pushed to be shaped to an exact size, then caressed between sweet white milk bread (similar to Japanese *shokupan*), which is toasted in butter until just about crisp. You can ask for a slice of American-style cheese to be added before the egg is topped with some more shredded cabbage. Then the whole thing gets doused in a generous sprinkle of sugar and tangy ketchup to balance and cut through the flavours in the most unassumingly delicious way. It's mesmerizing to watch the chef's hands move so harmoniously with the ingredients they are handling. I find it beautiful: gracefully systematic and rhythmical like a well-rehearsed dance that expresses the life lived through their hands.

MAKES 1

2 eggs
¼ tsp sea salt flakes
⅛ tsp ground white pepper
unsalted butter, for cooking
1 tsp golden granulated sugar
1 slice of cheese such as
    Port Salut, mild Cheddar
    or American cheese
2 slices of white bread
1 thick slice of sandwich ham
4 round slices of
    pickled gherkins
40g (½oz) white cabbage,
    thinly shredded
mayonnaise, to taste
tomato ketchup (catsup),
    to taste

Crack the eggs into a jug or bowl. Add the salt and white pepper and beat energetically to create smooth strands with no lumps.

Melt a small knob of butter in a non-stick frying pan (skillet) over a low heat and swirl it round to coat the pan evenly. When the butter has melted, pour the whisked egg into the pan. As the egg starts to spread around the pan, start dragging the cooked edges decisively towards you, while tilting the pan slightly to let the uncooked egg run away to cook – we are aiming to make a quick, barely set egg somewhere between scrambled and an omelette. Gather and fold the egg on itself to maintain the shape and size of the bread. The eggs should appear almost cooked in under 30 seconds. Flip carefully and briefly cook the other side. Transfer to a plate, sprinkle with the sugar and top with the cheese. Keep warm.

Wipe down the pan with kitchen paper, if necessary, and melt another small knob of butter. Place in both slices of bread to toast, adding more butter to the pan as necessary. Flip frequently to toast evenly. Once the bread is golden and lightly crispy, remove from the pan and allow to cool a little.

To assemble the sandwich, place the cheese-topped omelette on top of the first slice of toasted bread, followed by the slice of ham, the pickles and cabbage. Top with a generous dollop of mayonnaise and ketchup. Cover with the second slice of toast. Slice in half, if you like, and serve warm.

Potato Salad Sandwich

Gamja Salad Sandwich

My lovely Dutch friend often teases me when I express my dislike of sandwiches as a meal; for me, sandwiches are a snack that fills the gaps in between meals. This reluctance stems from experiences of sadly filled, dry, cold, stale bread that came as an afterthought emergency meal on the road, which often made me feel unsatisfied and deflated. But, of course, as with my obsession with *gimbap* – which encompasses anything and everything inside of perfectly seasoned savoury rice – I do appreciate the convenience of a sandwich and its tactile nature, which allows me to 'feel' what I am eating. When I eat with my hands, the texture I feel between my fingertips translates into flavour in my mouth, imparting a real sense of pleasure.

This is a good sandwich, loved by many Koreans, filled with a typical Korean creamy potato salad mashed up with boiled egg. It's squishy and creamy. I like to layer mine with very thin slices of salted cucumber to add a bit of bite. There is a smear of strawberry jam that I am sure will make you raise your eyebrows with concern, but a mashed potato salad sandwich with jam on pillow-soft white bread is what I would often eat for breakfast when I first came to London. Interestingly, though, this very combination of potato salad sandwich with jam has recently become popular among the K-pop stars. Who knew?!

MAKES 6 TEA SANDWICHES WITH A LITTLE LEFTOVER FILLING

150g (5oz) cucumber, sliced into thin rounds
sea salt flakes
4 slices of white sandwich bread (I like Japanese milk bread)
strawberry jam, to taste
salted butter at room temperature, for spreading

For the potato filling
200g (7oz) floury potatoes, peeled and quartered
sea salt flakes
2 hard-boiled eggs
20g (¾oz) onion, finely minced
20g (¾oz) pickled gherkins, finely diced
3 tbsp mayonnaise
2 tsp gherkin juice
1 tsp golden granulated sugar
1 tsp Dijon mustard
a pinch of ground white pepper

Put the cucumbers in a mixing bowl and toss lightly with a generous pinch of salt. Leave to stand for 10 minutes, then drain. Squeeze the drained cucumbers lightly by hand to remove any excess moisture. Set aside.

Put the potatoes in a large, lidded saucepan and cover with cold water to come 2cm (¾in) above the potatoes. Add a good pinch of salt, cover with the lid and bring to the boil. Turn down the heat and simmer gently for 10–15 minutes, or until the potatoes are cooked through. When done, drain and leave to cool slightly.

Meanwhile, separate the yolks from the whites of the hard-boiled eggs. Mash the yolks with a fork and finely mince the egg whites with a knife.

Once the potato has cooled enough to handle, transfer it to a large mixing bowl and mash with a fork; they don't need to be completely smooth. Stir in the prepared eggs. Add the onion, pickled gherkins, mayonnaise, gherkin juice, sugar, mustard and a pinch of white pepper, to taste. Give it a good mix to incorporate everything together. Taste and adjust the seasoning with a good pinch of salt, then add a touch more sugar or mustard, if you like.

To assemble the sandwich, lay all four slices of bread on the work surface. Spread a thin layer of jam onto the first two slices of bread. Spread a thin layer of butter on the other two. Put the potato salad mix generously between the two jam-smeared slices, spreading gently across. Top each with cucumber slices and cover with the buttered slices of the bread.

To serve, cut the crusts off the sandwiches, if you like, and slice each sandwich into three to make tea sandwiches.

Bunsik

Despite the literal translation being 'flour food' or 'food made with flour', bunsik nowadays generally refers to inexpensive snacks sold by street-food vendors or bunsik cafés.

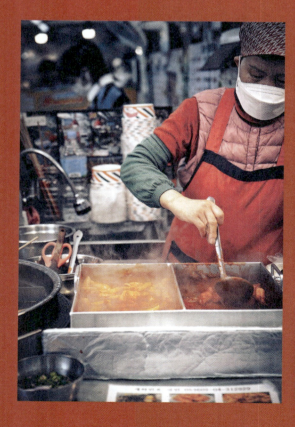

Ham + Coleslaw Fried Bun

Yetnal Salad Ppang

It is believed that the wide distribution of cooking oil in the 1970s may have strongly influenced the fried version of this dish, as the common assumption is that originally the bun was a soft bread roll. Here, a tender, crumbed sweet bun is fried, then filled with creamy coleslaw and finished with a good squirt of tangy tomato ketchup, with a great contrast in texture between the soft bun and the crunchy cabbage. It's sweet, tangy and salty with a subtle touch of mustard humming quietly in the background.

MAKES 8 BUNS

35g (1¼oz/⅔ cup)
 panko breadcrumbs
vegetable oil, for frying
American mustard, to taste
16 slices of cucumber
8 slices of sandwich ham

For the dough
125ml (4½fl oz/½ cup)
 full-fat milk
2 tbsp golden caster
 (superfine) sugar
½ tsp fine sea salt
200g (7oz/1⅔ cups)
 strong bread flour
50g (2oz/heaped ¼ cup)
 glutinous rice flour
1 tsp fast active yeast
 (quick yeast)
1 egg, lightly whisked
40g (1½oz) unsalted
 butter, cubed and
 at room temperature

For the coleslaw
150g (5oz) white cabbage
40g (1½oz) carrot, julienned
2 tbsp chopped pickled
 gherkins
2 tbsp mayonnaise
½ tsp golden granulated
 sugar
1 tbsp tomato ketchup
 (catsup), plus extra
 for garnish
sea salt flakes, to taste
freshly cracked black
 pepper, to taste

To make the dough, pour the milk into a small saucepan and gently warm until it reaches about 40°C (104°F). Remove from the heat and whisk in the sugar and salt to dissolve. Leave to cool slightly.

Meanwhile, combine both the flours and the yeast in a mixing bowl or the bowl of a stand mixer fitted with a dough hook. Slowly pour in the warm milk and sugar mixture. Stir to combine, using a wooden spoon or chopsticks if mixing by hand. Stir in the egg. Start bringing everything together by gently kneading to form a rough dough – it should take about 5 minutes. The dough will feel quite wet to start with but it will come together. If mixing by hand, I find the 'slap and fold' technique works particularly well here – if you're not familiar with this method, do search online as there are plenty of video tutorials available.

Gradually, add the soft cubed butter to the dough and knead energetically to combine for 10–15 minutes by hand, or 8–10 minutes in the stand mixer, until the butter is evenly incorporated into the dough. The dough may feel slightly tacky to touch and that is perfectly fine. Shape the dough into a large ball and transfer into a lightly greased bowl. Cover and rest it in a warm place for 1–1½ hours until doubled in volume.

Line a baking tray with parchment paper. Once the dough has risen, gently push down the middle to knock the air out. Transfer the dough onto a sturdy surface (there is no need to flour the surface as the dough is enriched with butter). Divide the dough into eight roughly equal pieces – each should weigh around 55g (2oz). Start working on one piece to form a round ball. I like to do this by cupping the dough ball against the work surface with my dominant hand and gently rotating my hand anti-clockwise while applying a gentle yet firm pressure to shape it into a tight ball with a smooth and supple surface. Repeat with the remaining dough.

Place the dough balls on the lined baking tray, making sure they are evenly spaced. Cover and rest in a warm place for 15 minutes.

Have a bowl of room-temperature water ready. Fill a shallow, rimmed dish or tray with the breadcrumbs and spritz them with a little water to moisten. Working one at a time, carefully dip the dough balls in the water, then roll onto the breadcrumbs to coat the surface. Transfer back to the lined baking tray, evenly spaced. Cover and leave to rest for a further 30 minutes until the dough has risen slightly again in volume.

Recipe continues overleaf

Meanwhile, make the coleslaw filling. Prepare the cabbage by removing any wilted outer leaves and the core. Using a sharp knife, mandoline or vegetable peeler, slice the cabbage into very fine strands. Transfer the shredded cabbage to a large mixing bowl and soak in cold water for 10 minutes. Drain well, then return to the (now dry) bowl. Add the rest of the filling ingredients and combine well to incorporate everything together. Check the seasoning and adjust it with salt, pepper, or a pinch more sugar. Cover and refrigerate until needed.

Prepare a cooling rack set over a roasting tray.

Fill a large, heavy-based saucepan with enough vegetable oil to submerge the dough balls but come no more than three-quarters of the way up the pan. Heat the oil to 170°C (340°F). Carefully lower a few of the dough balls into the pan, making sure you don't overcrowd the pan. Fry for 4 minutes, gently pushing them down and flipping them so they cook evenly, as the dough will continuously float to the surface. After 4 minutes, the buns should appear rich golden brown and cooked through. Transfer to the cooling rack. Continue with the remaining dough balls, then leave the buns to cool completely.

Using a sharp bread knife, slice the cooled buns down the middle about two-thirds of the way in, but not all the way through. Smear a thin layer of mustard inside – both top and bottom. Layer the bun with two slices of cucumber and a slice of ham, then fill it with the coleslaw, leaving the ragged open edges on show. Squirt some tomato ketchup on top, if you wish, and eat immediately.

Gochugaru-Glazed Spam Mini Gimbap

Kkoma Gimbap

Gwanjang Market in Seoul is the home of many stalls famously known for a freshly rolled mini rice roll called *mayak gimbap*, which literally translates as 'drug *gimbap*'. I can only assume it acquired the name because it is so highly addictive! It is usually filled with finely shredded sautéed carrots, strips of pickled radish and egg, but the combination of filling can be much more imaginative depending on where you sample the dish. The unassumingly simple, bite-sized morsels are served with a mustard-based dipping sauce; together it forms quite an unexpected harmony of flavours. My version here proudly deviates from the norm and opts for a mixture of piquant pickled chillies and spicy *gochugaru*-glazed salty-sweet Spam.

MAKES 12 SMALL ROLLS

3 sheets of seaweed, 18×20cm (7×8in)
12 pickled chillies (such as guindilla peppers)

For the dipping sauce
1 tsp golden caster (superfine) sugar
1 tsp English mustard
1 tsp soy sauce
1 tsp cider vinegar
1 tsp water

For the Spam
200g (7oz) can of Spam
1 tsp vegetable oil, for frying
2 tsp golden granulated sugar
2 tsp mirin
2 tsp soy sauce
1 tsp *gochugaru* (Korean red pepper flakes)
2 tbsp water

For the rice
300g (10½oz/1½ cups) warm, freshly cooked short-grain white rice
2 tsp toasted sesame oil, plus extra for brushing
1 tsp toasted white sesame seeds, lightly crushed, plus extra for garnish (optional)
1 tsp sea salt flakes

Fold the seaweed sheets in half, then fold again the opposite way. Cut along the lines with sharp scissors so you have 12 equal-sized rectangles. Set aside.

Make the dipping sauce by mixing together all the ingredients in a bowl, ensuring the sugar and mustard are thoroughly blended. Set aside until needed.

To prepare the Spam, slice the block lengthways into four equal-sized rectangular pieces measuring about 5×9cm (12×3½in) and 1cm (½in) thick. Cut each piece lengthways into four equal-sized batons so you have 16 in total. The batons should be about the same width (9cm/3½in) as the seaweed sheets.

Heat the oil in a frying pan (skillet) over a medium heat and fry the Spam batons until lightly browned on all sides. Lower the heat, add the sugar and mirin to the pan and cook for 1 minute, gently shaking the pan as the sugar starts to bubble and melt in and around the Spam. Pour in the soy sauce around the edges of the pan, swiftly followed by the *gochugaru* and water. Give it a gentle stir to bring everything together and cook over a low heat for 2–3 minutes to reduce the sauce. The Spam should be beautifully caramelized. Remove from the pan and set aside.

Put all the ingredients for the rice into a large bowl. Using a rice paddle or spatula, stir to coat each grain of rice with the seasoning without mushing the rice. The rice should cool slightly; enough to handle comfortably with bare hands.

To roll the mini *gimbap*, have a small bowl of water nearby and place a sheet of seaweed on a chopping board shiny-side down with a short edge facing you. Scoop about 25g (¾oz) of rice onto the seaweed. Dip your fingertips into the water and start spreading the rice over the seaweed. The rice layer doesn't need to be thick or neat – just be sure to leave a little border at the far end.

Place one piece of glazed Spam and a pickled chilli on top of the rice, about 1cm (½in) away from the short edge closest to you. Gently lift the edges of seaweed closest to you and, in one smooth motion, confidently lift the edge and fold to encase the filling, then tightly roll away from you until you reach the end. You may want to brush a little water at the end to help the seaweed stick. Repeat the process until you have 12 seaweed rolls.

Brush the finished rolls with a little sesame oil and sprinkle with a few sesame seeds, if you like. Slice the rolls into three small bite-sized pieces, wetting the blade of a sharp knife with some water as you go, to keep the slices nice and clean. *Gimbap* is best eaten fresh so serve immediately with any remaining glazed Spam and the dipping sauce on the side.

Inside-Out Seaweed Rice Roll with Smoked Mackerel + Perilla Leaves

Nude Gimbap

Back in the 90s, when there was a real boom of low-key *gimbap* cafés across Korea, tuna mayonnaise layered with fragrant perilla leaves became a highly popular choice, especially with these inside-out *gimbap* inspired by Californian rolls. Many places offered different filling options with contrasting flavour and texture combinations, taking advantage of its highly customizable nature.

I've always loved the convenience of *gimbap*, due to the fact that you can *gimbap* anything in much the same way as you can sandwich anything between two slices of bread. Chunky, flaked hot smoked mackerel dressed with zingy horseradish cream is a combination that pays homage to tuna mayo, with a little nod to smoked mackerel pâté. The anise-laced freshness of perilla leaves cuts through the richness and bolts everything together to turn it into one moreish bite.

MAKES 4 ROLLS

4 sheets of seaweed,
 18×20cm (7×8in)
16 perilla leaves
four 1×20cm (½×8in) long
 batons of *danmuji* (Korean
 sweet pickled radish)

For the cucumber
250g (9oz) cucumber
½ tsp sea salt flakes
½ tsp golden granulated
 sugar

For the carrots
1 tbsp extra virgin olive oil
200g (7oz) carrots, julienned
sea salt flakes, to taste

For the smoked mackerel
2 tbsp crème fraîche
 (or natural yogurt)
1 tbsp strong horseradish
 cream
½–1 tsp wasabi paste,
 depending on the
 strength
½ tsp freshly cracked
 black pepper
½ tsp golden granulated
 sugar
zest of 1 lemon and juice
 of ½ lemon
150g (5oz) hot
 smoked mackerel
sea salt flakes, to taste

To prepare the cucumber, cut it in half lengthways and scrape out the seeds with a teaspoon. Using a vegetable peeler, peel the cucumber halves into thin strips. Transfer to a mixing bowl and combine with the salt and sugar. Leave to sit for 20 minutes, then drain. Squeeze as much water out as you can by hand and pat dry with a dish towel to remove excess moisture. Set aside.

To prepare the carrots, heat the olive oil in a frying pan (skillet) over a medium heat. Add the carrots with a good pinch of salt and sauté gently for about 2 minutes. You should notice the tint of deep orangey-yellow seeping into the oil and smelling quite fragrant. Remove from the heat when the carrots appear softened. Set aside.

To prepare the smoked mackerel, whisk together the crème fraîche, horseradish cream, wasabi paste, black pepper, sugar, and lemon zest and juice in a large bowl. Peel the skin off the smoked mackerel fillets and roughly break up the flesh into large flakes into the mixing bowl, ensuring there are no small bones. Toss lightly to dress the mackerel with the sauce, then season with salt.

Place the warm, freshly cooked rice into a large mixing bowl, along with sesame oil, sesame seeds, *yondu* and salt. Using a rice paddle or spatula, stir energetically to coat each grain of rice with the seasoning without mushing the rice. The rice should cool slightly; enough to handle comfortably with bare hands. Check for seasoning and add a pinch more salt, if necessary.

To roll the inside-out *gimbap*, lay a piece of clingfilm (plastic wrap) slightly bigger than the size of the seaweed sheets on a chopping board and have a small bowl of water nearby. The clingfilm will provide stability and help you roll more easily. Place a sheet of seaweed on the clingfilm with a short edge nearest to you. Scoop 150g (5oz) of rice onto the middle of the seaweed. Dip your fingertips in the water, then start spreading the rice as evenly as possible, pinching and pressing it firmly onto the seaweed, leaving a 2.5cm (1in) gap on the bottom edge closest to you. Make sure you spread the rice to the full width of the sheet.

Recipe continues overleaf

For the rice

600g (1lb 5oz/5 cups)
    freshly cooked white
    short-grain rice
1 tbsp toasted sesame oil,
    plus extra for brushing
1 tbsp toasted white sesame
    seeds, lightly crushed
1 tsp *yondu* (seasoning
    sauce)
1 tsp sea salt flakes

Flip the rice-covered seaweed, so that the plain seaweed side faces upwards and the rice faces downwards. Arrange the fillings about 1cm (½in) away from the edge closest to you, beginning with the sheets of perilla leaves laid flat so that the rest of the fillings can be arranged on top. Put the cucumbers on top at the nearest end, followed by the smoked mackerel, carrots and *danmuji*.

Position both hands over the filling, with your thumbs gently lifting the clingfilm next to the edges of the seaweed closest to you. In one smooth motion, confidently lift the edge and fold to encase the filling, pressing down the edges firmly so the rice on the outside sticks to the seaweed. Just be confident with the first lift and tuck; think of rolling a sheet of paper into a tight tube. Tuck everything in firmly with a gentle cupping motion, and keep pressing down with your fingertips on the edges you have just folded. It should feel quite firm. Then roll with the same cupping motion until you reach the end. Repeat the process until you have four seaweed rolls.

Brush the finished rolls with a touch of sesame oil, if you like. Cut the rolls into small bite-sized slices 1.5cm (⅝in) thick, wetting the blade of a sharp knife with a little water as you go, to keep the slices nice and clean. *Gimbap* is best eaten fresh so serve immediately.

DANMUJI

Korean sweet pickled radish, called *danmuji*, can be found in Korean supermarkets, sold whole or cut into perfectly sized batons for making *gimbap*.

Northern-Style Kimchi Dumpling

Ibuksik Kimchi Mandu

My paternal grandfather was from North Korea and I grew up dutifully making these northern-style kimchi dumplings with my family as long ago as I can remember. My father insisted on practising the technique religiously for every family gathering or national holiday – large or small – in an effort to hold onto his roots. He was passionate about food, and some of these dishes were a small but important part of the family history he felt compelled to preserve, and which has now become my own family tradition here in London.

Northern-style dumplings are unadorned and typically bulked out with tofu to yield the flavour that is commonly described as *dambaekhan mat*, which loosely translates as clean, almost plain-tasting. Simply seasoned only with salt and pepper, the humbly balanced, unfussy filling lends an overall harmony of flavours. This recipe is an adaptation of my family's beloved dumpling recipe, respectfully furnished with more universal measurements translated from the original oral or visual descriptions such as 'thumbnail sized', 'one fistful', 'just enough', 'a touch more' or 'as you please'. I adore its decisively simple and honest taste. I hope you do, too.

MAKES AROUND 46 DUMPLINGS

2 x packs of 23 frozen dumpling wrappers (8cm/3¼in in diameter), defrosted in the fridge overnight
1 egg, lightly whisked

For the dumpling filling
150g (5oz) beansprouts
150g (5oz) firm tofu
250g (9oz) kimchi, drained
300g (10½oz) minced (ground) pork, preferably 20% fat
4 spring onions (scallions), finely minced
2 tsp toasted sesame oil
1 tsp freshly cracked black pepper
1 tsp golden granulated sugar
½ tsp sea salt flakes

For the dipping sauce
2 tbsp soy sauce
2 tbsp rice vinegar
2 tbsp water
2 tsp golden granulated sugar

To make the filling, bring a pan of salted water to the boil and have a bowl of cold water close by. When the water is rapidly boiling, carefully drop in the beansprouts and blanch them for 3 minutes until a little floppy. Using tongs or a wire skimmer, transfer the beansprouts to the bowl of cold water, then drain. Gently squeeze the water out of the beansprouts as much as you can by hand without squashing them. Chop the beansprouts as finely as you can, then transfer to a large mixing bowl big enough to accommodate the rest of the filling ingredients, or into the mixing bowl of a stand mixer, if you have one.

Wrap the block of tofu in a piece of muslin or cheesecloth and wring it as tightly as you can to remove the excess water. The tofu inside will crumble as you squeeze and twist, and this is perfectly fine. Add to the mixing bowl with the beansprouts and set aside.

To prepare the kimchi, ensure it is well drained by gently squeezing to remove the excess moisture. Finely chop and add to the mixing bowl.

Pat the pork dry with kitchen paper to remove any sitting blood and add to the mixing bowl, along with the spring onions.

Add the sesame oil, black pepper, sugar and salt and work the mixture energetically with your hands to combine, as if you are kneading dough, scraping the edges in a scooping motion to thoroughly mix everything together. As you work the mixture, it will start to feel almost sticky. If you are using a stand mixer, use the paddle attachment and process for a couple of minutes until well combined.

Line a couple of baking trays with parchment paper, so you can transfer the shaped dumplings as you go. Set up a comfortable working station: have ready the lined trays, dumpling wrappers, a bowl with the whisked egg, and the filling mixture. I like to do this seated at the table so that my family and/or friends can get involved in the communal activity of shaping the dumplings together.

Recipe continues overleaf

To shape the dumplings, place a wrapper on the palm of your non-dominant hand. Dip the index fingertip of your dominant hand into the whisked egg and rub it gently but thoroughly along the outer edge of the wrapper; this will ensure the finished dumpling is sealed securely.

Place a heaped teaspoonful of filling – or slightly less, if you're finding it tricky to handle – at the centre of the wrapper, pressing firmly to ensure it is well packed. Bring the bottom and top edges together to fold into a half-moon shape, making sure you press the edges firmly to seal securely. You may want to push the filling in a bit as you move along the edges. Once sealed, bring both corners to meet in the middle, overlapping the ends. Rub a little egg in between and press firmly together to seal. Transfer to the lined tray. Continue working through the rest of the dumplings.

Make the dipping sauce by mixing all the sauce ingredients together.

To cook the dumplings, you can either steam them over a medium heat for 11 minutes or simmer for 5 minutes by plunging them into a pan of boiling water. Serve warm with the dipping sauce on the side.

Leftover cooked dumplings can be stored in the fridge for 3 days or for a couple of months in the freezer.

DUMPLING WRAPPERS

For the convenience of this recipe, I am using shop-bought dumpling wrappers found in the freezer section in Korean supermarkets. If you wish to make the wrappers yourself, you can do so by combining 300g (10½oz/2⅓ cups) of plain (all-purpose) flour with 150ml (5fl oz/scant ⅔ cup) water and a pinch of salt to make the dough, then roll into a 10cm (4in) wide disc, each weighing about 15g (½oz). There are plenty of video tutorials available online. The filling here is enough to fill about 30 homemade wrappers.

Soup Tteokbokki

Gukmul Tteokbokki

Tteok means rice cake and *bokki* comes from a Korean word meaning stir to cook, with or without oil. *Tteokbokki* started its journey as a royal court dish; rice cakes simmered with beef strips in a soy sauce-based seasoning used to be a dish served only to aristocrats. The original dish is commonly known as *gungjung tteokbokki* or *ganjang tteokbokki*. Since then, many variations of the dish have been made to cater for Koreans' love of toothsome rice cakes, from extremely hot *gochujang*-based sauce to salty-sweet *chunjang* (Korean black bean sauce) to creamy cheesy sauce; the choices really are almost endless. And *tteokbokki* remains one of the best-loved street snacks in Korea, with everyone having their own personal favourite.

The recipe here is a soupy version in which the sauce is runny enough to be enjoyed with a spoon. The dish has a warming heat but is not overly spicy, ensuring a balanced salty-sweet finish.

SERVES 2

300g (10½oz) cylinder-shaped rice cakes (fresh or frozen)
150g (5oz) frozen fishcakes (any shape works fine)
125g (4oz) white cabbage, roughly sliced into large bite-sized pieces
4 spring onions (scallions), cut into 5cm (2in) batons
freshly cracked black pepper, to taste

For the sauce
½ onion, sliced
2 tbsp golden granulated sugar
1 tbsp *yondu* (seasoning sauce)
1 tbsp fish sauce
1 tbsp soy sauce
1 tbsp *gochujang* (Korean fermented chilli paste)
1 tbsp *jocheong* (rice syrup) or clear honey
1 tsp *gochugaru* (Korean red pepper flakes)
400ml (13fl oz/1½ cups) just-boiled water

If you are using frozen rice cakes, soak them in cold water for 10 minutes to soften first. When ready, drain and set aside.

To make the sauce, put the onion, sugar, *yondu*, fish sauce, soy sauce, *gochujang*, *jocheong*, *gochugaru* and water into a wide sauté pan or saucepan and stir to combine. Bring to the boil, then simmer for 5 minutes over a medium heat.

Meanwhile, plunge the frozen fishcakes in warm water for 1 minute. Drain and slice into bite-sized pieces.

Stir the rice cakes, fishcakes, white cabbage and spring onions into the pan with the sauce. Season liberally with black pepper. Bring to a high simmer and continue simmering over a medium heat for 5 minutes. Check that the rice cakes are cooked; they should feel soft and tender. If they require a few more minutes, reduce the heat to low and continue cooking for a couple more minutes until done. When ready, remove from the heat and enjoy while still warm.

FISHCAKES

Korean fishcakes can be found in the freezer section in most Asian stores. They come in various shapes, from more common flat square sheets to round balls – any shape works perfectly fine here.

Oil Tteokbokki with Chilli Crisp + Honey

Gireum Tteokbokki

This oily version of *tteokbokki* is believed to have appeared in the markets in Seoul after the Korean War in the early 1950s. The dish is thought to have its roots in the northern style of cooking and is considered to be more reminiscent of original *gungjung tteokbokki*, as earlier iterations were seasoned only with soy sauce or with very little use of *gochugaru*.

Frying the rice cakes should be done gently and with patience over a consistently low heat to allow the exterior of the chewy rice cakes to become crispy and deeply scorched; the burnished *gochugaru* balanced with caramelized sugar. Rush to cook them too fast and you will end up burning the *gochugaru* and making it unpleasantly bitter, so please take your time and care for the humble ingredients.

I rather inauthentically add chilli crisp to lace the dish with more lip-smacking heat. It's an impeccably simple dish that delivers the ultimate comfort of oily carbs, sugar and spice – what's not to like?

SERVES 2

300g (10½oz) cylinder-shaped rice cakes (frozen or fresh)
1 tbsp *gochugaru* (Korean red pepper flakes)
2 tbsp perilla oil
2 tbsp soy sauce
2 tsp golden granulated sugar
1 tbsp vegetable oil
2 spring onions (scallions), cut into 5cm (2in) batons, then julienned
1 tbsp chilli crisp (I like Chiu Chow chilli oil)
1 tbsp raw, clear honey
1 tsp toasted white sesame seeds, lightly ground

If you are using frozen rice cakes, soak them in cold water for 10 minutes to soften first.

Plunge the rice cakes in boiling water for 1 minute, then drain and rinse with cold water. Drain fully to remove any excess moisture, then toss together with the *gochugaru*, perilla oil, soy sauce and sugar in a large mixing bowl. Set aside until needed.

Have a plate lined with kitchen paper ready. Heat the vegetable oil in a wok or frying pan (skillet) over a medium heat and fry the spring onions until golden brown and crispy. You may need to tilt the pan a little to pool the oil to help the spring onions to fry. Remove the spring onions from the oil and transfer to the plate lined with kitchen paper. Set aside until needed. Keep the oil in the pan for the next step.

Add the seasoned rice cakes to the same pan you used to fry the spring onions. Fry gently over a low heat for about 8 minutes, stirring frequently, until the rice cakes appear crispy and scorched in places, and are cooked through and tender.

Stir in the chilli crisp and honey, and let the mixture bubble for 1–2 minutes to caramelize. Remove from the heat and transfer to a platter. Top with the fried spring onions and sprinkle with the sesame seeds. Eat while warm.

Crispy Seaweed Roll

Gimmari

This is the Korean street-food dish I crave the most! I know deep-frying can sometimes feel like such a faff – sorry – but I am such a sucker for fried food. The naturally briny umami flavour of seaweed that blankets slippery noodles, is the understated star that makes this dish so special. Lightly seasoned noodles lifted with a gentle touch and almost floral aroma of white pepper, the simple flavours and textures come together so harmoniously. It is such an addictive bite, especially when served alongside *tteokbokki* (page 73).

MAKES 9 ROLLS

3 sheets of seaweed,
  18×20cm (7×8in)
plain (all-purpose) flour,
  for dusting
vegetable oil, for
  deep-frying

For the filling
100g (3½oz) *dangmyeon*
  (Korean sweet potato
  vermicelli noodles)
30g (1oz) carrot, grated
1 spring onion
  (scallion), sliced
1 tbsp light or soup
  soy sauce
1 tsp toasted sesame oil
½ tsp golden granulated
  sugar
½ tsp ground white pepper
sea salt flakes, to taste

For the batter
4 tbsp rice flour
2 tbsp cornflour (cornstarch)
½ tsp sea salt flakes
a pinch of ground turmeric
  (optional)
80ml (3fl oz/⅓ cup)
  fridge-cold water

For the dipping sauce
1 tbsp soy sauce
1 tbsp rice wine vinegar
1 tbsp water
1 tsp golden granulated
  sugar
1 hot green chilli, sliced

Soak the *dangmyeon* in cold water for 20 minutes, then drain.

Make the dipping sauce by mixing together all the ingredients in a small bowl and combining well. Set aside until needed.

Bring a pan of water to the boil. When the water is rapidly boiling, drop in the pre-soaked noodles and cook according to the packet instructions. Once done, drain and rinse under cold water a few times, then drain fully. Use your hand to gently squeeze the water out of the noodles as much as you can. Roughly cut the noodles once or twice using kitchen scissors. Leave to stand in the colander for 5 minutes to dry out fully before transferring to a mixing bowl.

Add the rest of the filling ingredients to the mixing bowl and toss to combine, preferably by hand. Check the seasoning and adjust with more salt, if needed.

To form the seaweed rolls, place a sheet of seaweed on a chopping board shiny-side down with a longer edge nearest to you. Spread about one-third of the seasoned noodle mixture onto the seaweed, leaving a 1cm (½in) gap on the edge closest to you and a small gap on each side. Gently lift the closest edge of the seaweed and, in one smooth motion, confidently lift the edge and fold to encase the filling, tucking and pulling gently to keep it tight. Roll away from you until you reach the end. You may want to brush a little water at the end to help the seaweed stick. Transfer to a tray and repeat with the remaining ingredients.

Rest the rolls for 20 minutes at room temperature, during which time the noodles will swell and plump. Using kitchen scissors or a knife, cut each roll into three equal pieces (about 7cm/2¾in long). Lightly dust the rolls with plain flour.

Make the batter by combining both flours with the salt, and turmeric if using, in a mixing bowl. Gradually pour in the cold water, whisking to combine.

Prepare a cooling rack set over a roasting tray. Fill a large, heavy-based saucepan with enough vegetable oil to submerge the spring rolls but come no more than three-quarters of the way up the pan. Heat the oil to 170°C (340°F).

When the oil reaches the right temperature, using tongs or chopsticks, hold a flour-dusted seaweed roll firmly, plunge it in the batter and swish it around gently to coat. Don't worry if it's not looking smooth and even; it doesn't need to be thick. Carefully lower the batter-dipped roll into the pan, then do the same with the next roll. Fry each roll for 3 minutes, gently moving them around to keep them separate and making sure you don't overcrowd the pan. Once each roll is lightly golden (rice flour makes them remain relatively pale golden in colour) and cooked through, transfer it to the cooling rack to drain off any excess oil.

When all the rolls are cooked, serve warm with the dipping sauce (you can slice the rolls into even smaller bite-sized pieces, if you like).

DO TRY THIS
I highly recommend you enjoy these rolls with Soup Tteokbokki (page 73) so you can dip the rolls in *tteokbokki* sauce to experience the beautiful flavour combination.

Korean Croquette Triangles

Korokke Ppang

The name *korokke* is thought to originate from the Japanese spelling of the French *croquette*. Although very different, the Korean and Western versions share a mashed potato-based filling and a deep-fried breadcrumb coating. The Korean *korokke* has a filling wrapped in a yeasted dough before being dredged with breadcrumbs.

Making pinwheel pastries with my daughter the other day, it suddenly occurred to me that encasing the filling inside a buttery soft puff pastry might create a satisfying texture that mimics the crispy exterior and pillowy bite. With a touch of curry powder mildly spicing the filling, this version tastes much like the old-fashioned *korokke* I used to enjoy from the market, without the hassle of deep-frying.

MAKES 30 TRIANGLES

2 sheets of ready-rolled puff pastry
1 egg, lightly whisked with a pinch of salt
toasted black sesame seeds, to decorate

For the filling
200g (7oz) floury potatoes, peeled and quartered
sea salt flakes, to taste
2 tbsp vegetable oil
1 onion, finely diced
100g (3½oz) white cabbage, diced
60g (2oz) carrot, coarsely grated
1 tbsp mild curry powder
1 tsp golden granulated sugar
3 spring onions (scallions), sliced
3 tbsp mayonnaise
½ tsp freshly cracked black pepper

To make the filling, place the potatoes in a large, lidded saucepan and fill it with cold water to come about 2cm (¾in) above the potatoes. Add a good pinch of salt and bring to the boil. Cover with the lid, turn down the heat and simmer gently for about 15 minutes, or until the potatoes are cooked through. Drain and leave to cool slightly.

Heat the oil in a large frying pan (skillet) over a low heat. Add the onion, cabbage and carrot with a generous pinch of salt and sweat very gently for 10 minutes to soften the vegetables until they smell deliciously sweet and tender. Stir in the curry powder, sugar and spring onions. Cook briefly until blended, then remove from the heat and leave to cool slightly.

Once the potatoes have cooled down, transfer them to a large mixing bowl and mash with a fork; the mixture doesn't need to be completely smooth. Stir in the sautéed vegetables, then add the mayonnaise and black pepper and combine well to incorporate everything together. Check the seasoning and adjust it with a pinch of salt, if needed.

Cut each pastry sheet into 15 equal rectangles, measuring roughly 6.5×8cm (2½×3¼in) – the simplest way to do this is to cut the pastry sheet lengthways into three rows, then cut each row into 5 equal pieces. Line a baking tray with parchment paper.

Working one at a time, spoon a tablespoon of filling onto one half of a pastry rectangle at an angle, so that you can fold diagonally at the centre to make a triangular-shaped pasty. Press the filling to pack it down tightly. Fold diagonally and seal the edges securely, then crimp the edges with a fork. Transfer to the lined baking tray and continue working until you have used all the ingredients. Refrigerate for 10 minutes to chill.

Preheat the oven to 180°C fan (200°C/400°F/gas 6).

Lightly brush the pastry triangles with the whisked egg and sprinkle the tops with a pinch of black sesame seeds. Bake for 30 minutes in the middle of the oven until golden brown. Enjoy while warm, but they are also good cold.

Mozzarella Corn Dog

Cheese Hotdog

I think those, like me, who were born in the 80s will have fond memories of this after-school snack, which used to be sold in local stationery shops called *munbanggu*, where you could also buy cheap, low-quality sweets, books, pencils, toys and everything in between. Most of these spots near schools offered a few random freshly made snacks in the afternoon, and that often included these Korean hotdogs.

The old-school hotdog used to be double-dipped in batter and fried twice, which forms two visible layers inside that are unique to this original style of Korean hotdog. The suspiciously pink sausage in the middle was rather small, but the deep-fried doughnut-like batter was delightfully crispy and soft all at once, carrying the salty flavours of ham perfectly. Nowadays, it is usually dipped in batter only once. Dust the hotdog with sugar while hot and enjoy with vinegary ketchup to channel the retro vibe! It's a delicious little treat.

MAKES 8 LARGE CORNDOGS

8 sturdy wooden skewers
4 frankfurters, cut in half to make each piece about 7.5cm (3in) long
8 cubes of low-moisture mozzarella, about 1.5×2cm (⅝×¾in)
plain (all-purpose) flour, for dusting
60g (2oz/heaped 1 cup) panko breadcrumbs
vegetable oil, for frying

For the batter

225ml (8fl oz/1 cup) warm water
75g (3oz/scant ½ cup) golden caster (superfine) sugar
1 tsp fine sea salt
300g (10½oz/scant 2½ cups) strong white bread flour
1 tsp fast active yeast (quick yeast)
1 egg, lightly whisked

To finish

2 tbsp golden caster (superfine) sugar
tomato ketchup (catsup), to taste
American mustard, to taste (optional)

To make the batter, whisk together the water, sugar and salt in a jug with a pouring spout until the sugar and salt have dissolved.

Combine the flour and yeast in a mixing bowl. Slowly pour in the warm water and sugar mixture, followed by the egg. Stir to combine using a wooden spoon. Continue to work the mixture until everything is well incorporated and it forms a relatively smooth, elastic batter – it should take about 10 minutes by hand or less if using a stand mixer, which I recommend. Don't worry if there are a few lumps. The batter should feel wet and quite stretchy. Cover with clingfilm (plastic wrap) and rest it in a warm place for 45 minutes to 1 hour until doubled in volume.

Meanwhile, thread each skewer with a piece of frankfurter and mozzarella, starting with the frankfurter. Dust the skewers lightly with some plain flour on all sides.

You are going to shape and fry each corn dog one at a time, so once the batter has rested, set up a working station with the loaded skewers, the batter bowl, and the breadcrumbs on a large plate, preferably in that order. Have the sugar to finish ready on another plate and prepare a cooling rack set over a roasting tray.

Fill a large, heavy-based saucepan with enough vegetable oil to submerge the corn dogs but come no more than three-quarters of the way up the pan. Heat to 170°C (340°F).

To shape the first corn dog, hold the end of the loaded skewer in your dominant hand, plunge it into the batter and confidently rotate the skewer to coat the sausage and cheese. You may want to wet your non-dominant hand and use it to help with shaping. Don't worry if it's not looking smooth and even; just take your time to get a reasonable coverage, especially around the cheese. It doesn't need to be thick; as it fries, it will soon increase in volume. Lift the corn dog out of the batter and, swiftly and carefully, roll it in the breadcrumbs.

Carefully lower the corn dog into the pan and fry for 4–5 minutes until golden brown and cooked through, gently pushing it down with a heatproof sieve or wire skimmer if it floats up so that it fries evenly. Using tongs, transfer the corn dog to the cooling rack to drain the excess oil, then roll in the sugar while warm. Continue with the remaining corn dogs. When all the batches are cooked, serve immediately with a drizzle of ketchup and mustard, if you like.

SHAPING
THE HOTDOGS

I found shaping the hotdogs takes a bit of practice as the stretchy batter can be quite unruly. Some people prefer to work with the batter in a large, flat, rimmed tray to rotate the skewers, while others prefer to transfer the batter into a tall jug or jar so they can dip the skewers into the batter in one smooth motion. It may be worth experimenting to see which method suits you best.

LOW-MOISTURE
MOZZARELLA

This is a hard mozzarella block for melting, often labelled as for pizza.

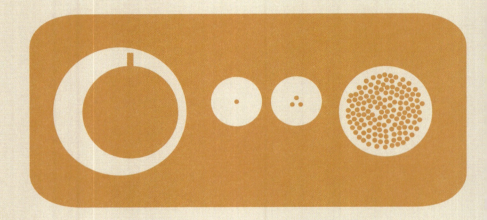

Everything Over Rice · Piquant Pickles + Salads on the Side

MARKET LUNCH

Everything Over Rice

Filling rice bowls inspired by the exuberant variety of produce and flavours from the markets of Seoul.

Ssambap with Doenjang Vegetables

Gang-Doenjang Ssambap

There are some dishes in Korean cuisine that I feel you may never get to experience properly unless you keenly explore the narrow streets beyond the trending hotspots on the map. This rather simple assembly of rice and stewed vegetables fits that bill perfectly.

A humble homestyle dish of fermented bean paste stew, it has a thick consistency. The deeply savoury and rounded salty flavour of *doenjang* seasons the sweet vegetables and binds the pearly grains of rice to deliver a comforting bite that swallows soothingly. Enjoy it with tender seasonal leaves, softly blanched, to wrap everything together to form a delicious bite-sized parcel. This is the real taste of Korea that deserves a place in the spotlight.

SERVES 4

½ tbsp vegetable oil
½ tbsp perilla oil
1 onion, diced
sea salt flakes, to taste
250g (9oz) mushrooms, diced into 1cm (½in) cubes (most types work here – try button, chestnut, shiitake or king oyster)
150g (5oz) courgettes (zucchini), diced into 1cm (½in) cubes
200g (7oz) potatoes, diced into 1cm (½in) cubes
2 garlic cloves, minced
250ml (8½fl oz/1 cup) just-boiled water
1 tsp *yondu* (seasoning sauce)
200g (7oz) firm or medium-set tofu, diced into 1cm (½in) cubes
1 hot or mild red chilli, chopped
1 hot or mild green chilli, chopped
1 spring onion (scallion), sliced

For the seasoning paste
2 tbsp *doenjang* (Korean fermented bean paste)
1 tbsp *gochujang* (Korean fermented chilli paste)
1 tsp *gochugaru* (Korean red pepper flakes)
½ tsp golden granulated sugar
½ tsp freshly cracked black pepper

To finish
4 servings of cooked short-grain white rice
blanched white cabbage leaves

Mix together all the ingredients for the seasoning paste and set aside.

Heat both the vegetable and perilla oils in a large, lidded, heavy-based saucepan. Add the onion and a pinch of salt, and sauté over a low–medium heat for 3–5 minutes to soften. Stir in the mushrooms with another pinch of salt and continue sautéing for 5 minutes, stirring frequently. You should notice the mushrooms collapsing as they cook down and release their moisture, and they will start to smell fragrant.

Add the courgettes and potatoes and stir briefly to combine. Lower the heat and stir in the seasoning paste, ensuring it is well incorporated with the vegetables. Continue cooking for 5 minutes, stirring occasionally.

Stir in the garlic, water, *yondu* and tofu. Bring to the boil, cover with a lid, then simmer gently over a low heat for 20 minutes to reduce and thicken the stew, stirring occasionally.

After 20 minutes, the stew will have very little liquid left, but it should still be moist enough to fall softly off the spoon. Check for seasoning and adjust it with a pinch more salt, if necessary. Stir in the chillies and spring onion. Remove from the heat and leave to stand for a couple of minutes.

Divide the stew among four bowls and serve alongside the rice and cabbage leaves, so you can wrap each spoonful of thickened vegetable stew and rice in the cabbage leaves.

Cubed Steak Deopbap

Cube Steak Deopbap

Cubed steak became a highly popular item in the ever-evolving Korean street-food scene, tickling the fancies of passers-by with theatrical displays of fire and delicious-smelling smoke. Toppings and side dishes to accompany the meat make it a satisfying meal on the go and can be anything from potatoes – think perfectly ball-shaped mash, hash browns or crinkled fries – to seasonal salads or melting cheese, inspired by exciting flavours from near and far.

The dish seems to have become a regular fixture of home cooking too, as it is a fairly quick and easy one-bowl dish. I particularly like this simple version using an onion-based sauce, which you cook in the same pan that the meat was seared in; I like to deglaze the pan with plenty of butter to maximize the rich, rounder-bodied sauce. The seasoning of salty-sweet soy sauce packs an uncomplicated yet luxurious punch that is friendly and familiar. It's a delicious supper that you can easily whip up on a weeknight, but it feels like a real treat.

SERVES 4

1 tbsp vegetable oil
1 tbsp mayonnaise
1 tsp golden granulated sugar
500g (1lb 2oz) beef steak (bavette, ribeye or sirloin)
sea salt flakes, to season

For the onion sauce
2 onions, thinly sliced
40g (1½oz) unsalted butter
4 tbsp mirin
4 tbsp water
4 tbsp sugar
4 tbsp soy sauce
2 tbsp Worcestershire sauce
2 tsp English mustard
½ tsp freshly cracked black pepper

To finish
4 servings of cooked short-grain white rice
a handful of salad cress, for garnish
chilli powder, to taste

Combine the vegetable oil, mayonnaise and sugar in a mixing bowl. Pat the beef dry with kitchen paper, then transfer it to the bowl. Massage well to coat the meat evenly.

Heat a heavy-based frying pan (skillet) until it is nice and hot; you want the steak to sizzle and caramelize as soon as it hits the pan. Season the steak generously with salt just before cooking and place it carefully into the hot pan. Sear the steak for a couple of minutes on each side, or to your preference. The timing of the steak will depend on the thickness of the meat, how hot the pan is and how you like your steak, so watch it carefully. Once done, transfer to a plate and leave to rest while you get on with the sauce.

Toss the onions into the same frying pan while reducing the heat immediately to medium. Add the butter and a little pinch of salt. Sauté the onions for about 3 minutes until they start to appear translucent and softened. Stir in the mirin and cook for 1 minute to reduce a little. Add the water, sugar, soy sauce, Worcestershire sauce, mustard and black pepper. Combine well and let it bubble for 5 minutes or so to thicken.

Meanwhile, slice the rested steak into 2cm (¾in) cubes. Any resting juices collected should be poured into the bubbling sauce. Check the sauce before removing from the heat and adjust the seasoning with a pinch more salt and pepper, if necessary. The sauce should be a pourable, syrupy consistency and appear beautifully glossy.

To assemble, divide the rice between four plates or bowls and top with the onions, reserving some of the sauce to finish the dish. Divide the cubed steaks evenly among the dishes and drizzle the reserved sauce on top. Top with some salad cress and a pinch of chilli powder. Enjoy while warm.

Spicy Stir-Fried Squid Deopbap

Ojingeo Deopbap

I've always adored the boldly spicy taste of this dish, which is balanced with just enough sweetness to offset the exuberant heat of smoky *gochujang* and *gochugaru*. Stir-fried quickly over a high heat, the speed in which it delivers the loud and fast flavours is both convenient and satisfying. The scored flesh of the squid holds the many flavours of the comfortingly unfussy sauce.

SERVES 2

200g (7oz) squid, fresh or thawed from frozen
1 tbsp vegetable oil
½ onion, sliced
3 spring onions (scallions), cut into 5cm (2in) batons
1 mild green or red chilli, sliced at an angle

For the seasoning

1 tbsp golden granulated sugar
1 tbsp *gochugaru* (Korean red pepper flakes)
1 tbsp mirin
1 tbsp *gochujang* (Korean fermented chilli paste)
2 tbsp soy sauce
2 tsp toasted sesame oil
½ tsp freshly cracked black pepper
3 garlic cloves, minced
½ tsp grated root ginger
sea salt flakes, to taste

To finish

2 servings of cooked short-grain white rice
toasted white sesame seeds
small handful of salad cress (optional)

Combine all the ingredients for the seasoning in a large mixing bowl big enough to accommodate the squid.

Open the tube of squid out flat by inserting a sharp knife inside to cut along the natural line. Once flat, scrape off any membranes and rinse the flesh under running water. Pat the squid dry with kitchen paper. Score the inside of the body in a criss-cross pattern with a sharp knife, ensuring the knife is only inserted about one-third of the way into the flesh at an angle. Cut into manageable widths and slice into bite-size rectangular strips. Cut the tentacles into similar-length pieces, if using. Repeat with the other squid, if appropriate.

Transfer the strips of squid to the mixing bowl with the seasoning and toss well to combine.

Heat the oil in a wok or frying pan (skillet) over a medium heat. Add the onion and spring onions and flash-fry for 2 minutes to soften. Increase the heat, then stir in the seasoned squid and the chilli. Cook for about 2 minutes until the squid is beautifully tender, stirring frequently to make sure the sauce doesn't catch on the base of the pan. The onion should still have a little bite but be tender enough to impart its natural sweetness. Once done, remove from the heat. Check the seasoning and adjust it with a pinch more salt or sugar, if necessary.

To serve, divide the rice between two bowls and generously ladle the warm, spicy squid on top. Scatter with the sesame seeds and some salad cress, if using. Enjoy while warm.

Spicy Tuna Mayo Rice Bowl

Gochu Chamchi Mayo Deopbap

I grew up obsessing over a particular brand of canned tuna, which was mildly spicy with a sweet edge. The oily, crimson red, *gochugaru*-stained sauce was considered a little greasy for some, but I liked how it silkily dressed the firm flakes of tuna. While a more traditional version includes a finely cubed medley of vegetables, I prefer to keep mine simple to build more focused flavour around the tuna. I love eating it smooshed over a bowl of rice, wrapping each spoonful with a salty-sweet toasted seaweed sheet to contrast the soft texture. It's good sandwiched between slices of bread, too, with some cheese melted in for extra oomph.

SERVES 2 GENEROUSLY

2 tbsp extra virgin olive oil
1 onion, finely diced
sea salt flakes, to taste
2 green chillies, chopped
1½ tbsp *gochugaru* (Korean red pepper flakes)
1 tbsp tomato paste
150g (5oz) can of tuna, drained
1 tbsp *gochujang* (Korean fermented chilli paste)
1 tbsp soy sauce
2 tsp golden granulated sugar
2 tsp Worcestershire sauce
½ tsp freshly cracked black pepper
100ml (3½fl oz/scant ½ cup) water

For the quick scrambled eggs
2 eggs
a pinch of sea salt flakes, to taste
1 tsp extra virgin olive oil

To finish
2 servings of cooked short-grain white rice
1 ripe avocado, cubed
mayonnaise, to taste (I like Japanese kewpie mayonnaise)
toasted black sesame seeds, for garnish
2 × 5g packs of toasted seaweed thins

Heat the olive oil in a sauté pan over a low heat. Add the onion and a generous pinch of salt and sweat very gently for 10 minutes to soften. When the onion has collapsed and is smelling sweet, stir in the green chillies, *gochugaru* and tomato paste and cook for 2 minutes, stirring frequently to make sure the *gochugaru* doesn't burn. You should notice the colour of the pastes staining the oil red.

Increase the heat a little and add the tuna, *gochujang*, soy sauce, sugar, Worcestershire sauce and black pepper. Give it a good stir to combine. Add the water and simmer gently for 5 minutes, stirring occasionally, until the sauce has reduced slightly and you have a thick consistency, like a ragù. Remove from the heat. Check for seasoning and adjust it with a pinch of salt, if necessary.

Meanwhile, make the quick scrambled eggs by whisking the eggs with the pinch of salt. Heat the olive oil in a wok over a medium heat and pour in the eggs. You should notice the edges of the egg mixture start to set. Using a chopstick or a spatula, pull the eggs towards you while tilting the pan away from you so that egg runs to the bottom. Repeat the technique until the eggs are almost set. In about 15 seconds, you should have very silky scrambled eggs. Remove from the heat and set aside.

To serve, divide the rice between two bowls and generously ladle the warm, spicy tuna over the rice. Top with the eggs, avocado and a squirt of mayonnaise. Scatter with black sesame seeds and serve with the toasted seaweed thins.

SEAWEED THINS

Seaweed thins are a toasted seaweed snack made from pressed seaweed. Korean seaweed thins are lightly brushed with oil (most commonly sesame oil mixed with vegetable, perilla or olive oil) and seasoned lightly with salt. They are then either dry toasted in a pan or, in some cases, grilled over a direct fire, until crispy. Often enjoyed as a healthy lunchbox snack, seaweed thins can be found in many supermarkets and health-food stores as well as Asian supermarkets. They are usually sold in multipacks.

Smoked Salmon Bibimbap

Hunje Yeoneo Hoe Deopbap

In Korea, raw fish is typically served with a bright vinegared *gochujang* dipping sauce. It is often eaten wrapped in pliable seasonal leaves to make *ssam*, so you can appreciate the diverse flavours in one harmonious bite, but it can also be enjoyed over a bowl of rice.

A beautifully zingy sauce combined with delicate fish and fragrant soft leaves, this recipe is actually a style of bibimbap but is more commonly known as *hoe deopbap*. It is a much lighter-tasting bowl, perfect on a hot summer's evening. I like to keep the toppings simple so there is no distraction from the piquant *gochujang* dressing on the smoked salmon, but you may like to choose alternative seasonal toppings or fresh sashimi-grade fish.

The dressing will benefit from being made in advance so the strong flavours can soften and further develop to yield a rounder finish. A squeeze of fresh lemon juice can also add a subtle citrus layer, though it isn't a must. Stored in an airtight container, it will keep well for about a week in the fridge; leftover dressing makes a great dipping sauce for steamed vegetables.

SERVES 2

¼ red onion, thinly sliced
100g (3½oz) smoked salmon, cut into bite-sized pieces
15 perilla leaves, sliced into thin strips
4 tbsp *gim jaban* (crumbled toasted seasoned seaweed)
½ punnet of cress

For the dressing
juice from 2 tsp grated root ginger
1 garlic clove, grated
3 tbsp cider vinegar
2 tbsp *gochujang* (Korean fermented chilli paste)
2 tbsp golden granulated sugar
2 tsp toasted sesame oil
1 tsp toasted white sesame seeds, lightly crushed

To finish
2 servings of cooked short-grain white rice
toasted black sesame seeds, for garnish

To make the dressing, put all the sauce ingredients in a mixing bowl. Combine well, cover and refrigerate until needed. I like to make this a day or two in advance to allow the flavours to soften and develop.

When ready to serve, soak the onion in cold water for 10 minutes to remove the harsh taste. Drain and set aside.

Divide the rice between two bowls. Arrange the smoked salmon, perilla leaves, *gim jaban*, cress and red onion in a visually pleasing way on top. Drizzle with some dressing to taste – for me, this is about 2 heaped tablespoons per bowl. Scatter with the black sesame seeds and serve with some extra sauce on the side.

Buttered Beansprout Rice

Kongnamulbap

When the need to cook fast outweighs the romantic aspects of cooking, the magic of a balanced one-pan dish that promises minimum effort and maximum taste sustains and rescues me time and time again. This is one of those brilliant dishes that is not only really easy to put together but good enough to perk up a lethargic appetite on a hot summer's day. You can't get enough of it!

Despite its simple appearance, the fragrant garlicky soy sauce dressing, spiked with cooling spring onions and *gochugaru*, complements the neutral taste of the steamed beansprouts and makes them taste nutty and sweet. Tender but still with a little crunch, the beansprouts add a refreshing texture that contrasts the soft, buttery rice, which puts me in mind of the buttered soy sauce rice I used to enjoy as a child. The dressing here is non-negotiable as it is what makes the dish sing, though you can, of course, dial up and down the garlic and chilli.

If you like, serve alongside roasted, seasoned seaweed sheets to wrap each spoonful like *ssam* for the ultimate experience of flavourful one-bite perfection.

SERVES 4

300g (10½oz/heaped 1½ cups) short-grain white rice
½ tbsp roasted sesame oil
½ tbsp vegetable oil
300ml (10fl oz/ 1¼ cups) water
30g (1oz) butter, cubed
300g (10½oz) beansprouts

For the beef
200g (7oz) minced (ground) beef
1 tbsp light or soup soy sauce
1 tbsp mirin
1 tsp roasted sesame oil
1 garlic clove, minced
¼ tsp freshly cracked black pepper

For the dressing
4 tbsp soy sauce
2 tbsp toasted sesame oil
1 tbsp *gochugaru* (Korean red pepper flakes)
1 tsp golden granulated sugar
1 tsp toasted white sesame seeds, lightly crushed
2 spring onions (scallions), thinly sliced
2 garlic cloves, grated
1 tsp finely chopped long red chilli

To finish
a handful of salad cress (optional)

Put the rice in a mixing bowl and wash thoroughly by swishing the grains or rubbing them between your hands until the water runs almost clear. Fill the bowl with cold water and let the rice soak for 30 minutes. When ready, drain the rice using a fine sieve and set aside.

Combine all the ingredients for the beef in a mixing bowl and leave to marinate for 10 minutes.

Make the dressing by combining all the dressing ingredients in a small bowl. Set aside until needed.

Heat both the sesame and vegetable oils in a heavy-based, lidded saucepan over a medium heat. Add the marinated beef and stir-fry for a few minutes until lightly browned, breaking up the grains with a spoon. Stir in the drained rice along with the water. Give it a good stir so the beef is well incorporated with the rice. Dollop the butter on top and put the lid on. Bring to the boil then immediately reduce the heat to low–medium and simmer for 10 minutes.

Turn the heat down as low as it can go. Add the beansprouts on top, put the lid back on and cook for a further 5 minutes to steam. Turn the heat off and leave to sit for 10 minutes with the lid firmly on. Carefully open the lid and give it a gentle stir with a rice paddle or wooden spoon. You will notice the slightly crunchy crust that has set beautifully on the bottom of the pan, which is absolutely delicious.

To serve, divide the rice into individual bowls, making sure each has a generous mixture of rice and beansprouts. Top with salad cress, if using, and enjoy it with liberal helpings of dressing stirred through. It is best eaten immediately.

Lamb Yuni Jjajang Sauce with Rice

Yuni Ijajangbap

Jjajang over rice is a homestyle dish. It's nothing fancy but makes a tasty, comforting meal that keeps everyone happy. *Yuni jjajang* – which is a variation of a Korean black bean sauce dish made with *chunjang* paste and minced meat – goes particularly well over rice, thanks to ingredients that are all diced finely and uniformly. Whenever I make it, I can't help but think of the similarities it shares with the rich Italian meat sauces such as Bolognese.

I cook this dish in a similar way to making ragù, in this case using lamb. The rich flavour of lamb mingles beautifully in the boldly salty-sweet sauce that is lightly spiced with a subtle hum of cinnamon and *gochugaru*. I like to keep my sauce a loose, fall-off-the-spoon consistency to bind the rice. Take time cooking the onions, as the dish relies on the rounded sweetness of the onion to support the bold flavour of salty and pungent black bean paste.

Serve with Turmeric Pickled Radish (page 110) or Spicy Pickled Radish Salad (page 114) to cut through the richness.

SERVES 4 WITH PLENTY OF LEFTOVERS

3 tbsp extra virgin olive oil
250g (9oz) onions, diced
4 garlic cloves, minced
sea salt flakes, to taste
400g (14oz) minced (ground) lamb
2 tsp grated root ginger
125g (4oz) *chunjang* (Korean black bean paste)
1 tbsp golden caster (superfine) sugar
2 tbsp soy sauce
2 tsp *gochugaru* (Korean red pepper flakes)
1 tsp ground cinnamon
1 tsp freshly cracked black pepper
600ml (20fl oz/2½ cups) just-boiled water
1 tbsp *yondu* (seasoning sauce)
1 tbsp oyster sauce

For the slurry
2 tbsp water
2 tbsp potato starch

To finish
4 servings of cooked short-grain white rice
125g (4oz) cooked frozen peas
4 fried eggs
¼ red onion, thinly sliced and soaked in cold water for 10 minutes, then drained
a pinch of fine chilli powder
toasted white sesame seeds

Heat the olive oil in a heavy-based saucepan over a low heat. Add the onions, garlic and a good pinch of salt to the pan and sauté for 15 minutes until the onions have completely collapsed and are smelling sweet and fragrant.

Increase the heat a little, add the lamb and ginger and continue cooking for 5 minutes, stirring frequently to break them up and colour evenly. You should notice the mince looking lightly brown and the fat from the lamb beautifully rendered. Turn down to a low heat, add the *chunjang* and stir vigorously to incorporate it into the onion and mince, then cook for about 3 minutes.

Add the sugar, soy sauce, *gochugaru*, cinnamon and black pepper and stir briefly to cook down the sugar. Stir in the water, *yondu* and oyster sauce. Bring just to the boil, then cover with a lid and simmer gently for 35 minutes, stirring occasionally, until the *jjajang* is glossily black with plenty of runny sauce.

Meanwhile, mix the water and potato starch to a slurry.

Maintaining the gentle heat, gradually stir in enough of the slurry to thicken the sauce slightly; you may not need it all. Cook for 3 minutes or so until all the ingredients are well incorporated. Check for seasoning and adjust it with a pinch more salt and sugar, if necessary.

To serve, divide the rice among four bowls and generously ladle the warm black bean sauce over the rice. Add the peas and top with the fried eggs, the red onion slices, a pinch of chilli powder and a sprinkling of toasted sesame seeds. Leftover sauce can be stored in an airtight container for up to 3 days in the fridge; it freezes well for up to 3 months.

Piquant Pickles + Salads on the Side

No Korean food experience is complete without banchan. Here is a small selection of simple recipes that are served in the markets to add some fresh flavours and textures on the side.

Stuffed Cucumber Kimchi

Oi Sobagi

Stuffed cucumber kimchi – often made to bridge the absence of winter kimchi – is enjoyed as soon as the warmth of spring hits Korea, utilizing the abundant cucumbers to capture the taste of the season. It tastes delightfully refreshing with subtly bitter-sweet onion flavours.

I use spring onions and chives for convenience, although this dish often uses garlic chives – so do use them if you can get them.

A pickling cucumber with bumpy skin is great for this dish, but an ordinary firm and slim cucumber works just fine too, as long as it is not full of seeds. I share a more traditional method of stuffing the cucumbers here, but do feel free to cut the cucumbers into batons, if you wish – salt the same way and just mix everything together instead of stuffing. Hot water salting might sound strange but is the key to retain the crisp texture of the cucumber, so do follow the steps below, including the shock of a cold shower that follows the brining.

MAKES ENOUGH TO FILL A 1.5 LITRE (56FL OZ/6¾ CUP) JAR OR EQUIVALENT

For the salting
1kg (2lb 4oz) pickling cucumbers (or use slim regular cucumbers)
1 litre (34fl oz/4 cups) water
2 tbsp coarse sea salt

For the kimchi filling
25g (1oz) garlic, roughly chopped
2 tsp roughly chopped root ginger
1 mild red chilli, roughly chopped
2 tbsp fish sauce
½ tsp shrimp paste
30g (1oz) *gochugaru* (Korean red pepper flakes)
1 tbsp Demerara sugar
½ onion, thinly sliced
3 spring onions (scallions), chopped
3 tbsp roughly chopped chives
½ tsp sea salt flakes, or to taste

Top and tail the cucumbers. (If using regular cucumbers, cut into batons about 5cm/2in long.) Halve the cucumbers lengthways but not all the way through to the bottom – about 1cm (½in) away from the base. Then rotate at 90° and do the same so you end up with criss-cross cut batons that open up. You should end up with something that looks a little like a four-legged octopus. Transfer the cut cucumbers to a large heatproof mixing bowl or container.

Bring the litre of water to the boil. Add the salt and whisk to combine. Pour the hot, salted water over the cucumbers and gently press them down to submerge; you may want to use a plate or lid on top to keep them under the brining water for 30 minutes.

Meanwhile, prepare the kimchi filling by blitzing together the garlic, ginger, red chilli, fish sauce and shrimp paste in a food processor until smooth. Transfer to a large bowl and stir in the *gochugaru* and sugar. Add both the onions, the chives and salt. Mix everything together, preferably by hand with gloves on, to combine. Check for seasoning and adjust it with a touch more salt, if necessary. It should taste slightly salty. Set aside.

After 30 minutes, drain the cucumbers. Rinse with cold water and drain again. Repeat the process a couple more times so that the cucumbers feel cool to the touch. Arrange the cucumber batons cut-side down in a large colander and leave to drain fully – this may take 15 minutes. Never squeeze the water out by hand.

Have a 1.5 litre (56fl oz/6¾ cup) jar or container for the kimchi ready. It doesn't need to be sterilized but should be thoroughly clean and bone dry.

Once the cucumbers are fully drained, working one baton at a time. Hold the base of the cucumber baton with your non-dominant hand right above the mixing bowl with the kimchi filling. Stuff a small amount of kimchi filling inside the open cavity, making sure the base stays intact. Once filled, squeeze the baton firmly to close and to remove any air pockets. Transfer to the jar or container as you go. Tightly pack but don't go fully up to the brim. Add any remaining filling to the top, then swish the bowl with 1 tablespoon of water, scrape off the paste and pour over the top of the cucumbers. Press down gently and cover with the lid.

The flavour of cucumber kimchi deepens after a day or two, so leave to sit at room temperature away from direct sunlight for a day, then transfer to the fridge to chill completely before serving. It will keep well for about a week in the fridge, without losing its crunchy texture.

Fresh Kimchi

Geotjeori

Geotjeori translates roughly as 'to salt lightly on the surface before seasoning'. This particular style of kimchi aims to retain the freshness of the vegetables to give the dish more of a salad-like quality than the robust depth of fermented kimchi. The dish is particularly popular in spring or summer when the fresh, leafy crops are young and tender enough to lend stimulating textures and lightness that contrast with an old winter kimchi. This one is eaten while fresh to enjoy the balanced flavour of zippy chilli heat and subtle sweetness, thus does not undergo the fermentation process.

The temptation to smother the salted cabbage in the mouthwatering heat of chillies is debatable, as some people prefer the dish quite boldly fiery, but I actually think the flavour of the sweet cabbage comes through better with a mild level of spiciness that gently tickles the palate.

Geotjeori does not keep all that well, as over time cabbage releases its natural moisture and loses its vibrancy. It is therefore best eaten fresh, hence the small quantity in this recipe.

It is delicious served alongside a bowl of steamed rice, doused generously with nutty roasted sesame oil to amplify the savouriness.

MAKES ENOUGH TO FILL A 1 LITRE (34FL OZ/4 CUP) JAR OR EQUIVALENT

1 Chinese cabbage, about 650g (1lb 7oz)
4 tbsp coarse sea salt
1 litre (34fl oz/4 cups) water
½ onion, thinly sliced
1 carrot, julienned
4 spring onions (scallions), chopped
4 garlic cloves, minced
1 tsp grated root ginger
4 tbsp *gochugaru* (Korean red pepper flakes)
3 tbsp fish sauce
1 tbsp plus 1 tsp golden granulated sugar
1 tsp toasted white sesame seeds

To prepare the cabbage, remove any wilted green outer leaves. Make a cut in the base of the cabbage then gently pull it apart in half lengthways to tear the leaves. Remove the cores and cut diagonally into bite-sized pieces. Transfer the cut cabbage to a large mixing bowl or container.

Combine the salt and water and whisk well until the salt has fully dissolved. Pour over the cabbage and press gently to submerge; you may want to use a plate to keep the cabbage under the water. Cover and leave to brine for 1 hour, flipping the top and bottom halfway through to ensure even salting, until the cabbage has softened.

Drain well, then rinse with fresh water and drain again. Repeat the process two more times so that you have thoroughly cleaned the cabbage. Leave to drain fully – this may take 30 minutes. Never squeeze the water out by hand as it will damage the structure of the cabbage and spoil the texture.

Once drained thoroughly, transfer to a large mixing bowl or container. Add the rest of the ingredients, except the sesame seeds, and gently massage everything together by hand (with gloves on) to combine. Check for seasoning and adjust it with a pinch more salt, if necessary. Toss in the sesame seeds.

Serve immediately or transfer to an airtight container to store in the fridge for up to 5 days.

Turmeric Pickled Radish

Danmuji

Traditionally, this bright, luminous, yellow pickled radish is made by burying air-dried radishes with rice bran and salt, along with the colouring, which is extracted from fruits of *Gardenia jasminoides Ellis*. As it begins its slow fermentation process, more water is released from the radishes, transforming its usual snappy crunchiness into an almost dry yet pleasantly chewy texture. The flavour is deep and boldly salty with a hard-to-detect, subtle sweetness lingering vaguely in the background.

However, the industrialization of production means that nowadays most, though not all, of the *danmuji* we eat has become reliant on a vinegar and sugar solution-based pickle. It is much sweeter, with a sour character leading the flavour profile, rather than salty. This modern process seems to translate well to a domestic kitchen set-up, too. Many home cooks have adopted the simple and less time-consuming pickling method, as I have here, which focuses on getting a texture similar to the more traditional version. I think it results in a good balance between a satisfying crunch and piquancy.

MAKES 1 LITRE (34FL OZ/4 CUP)

800g (1lb 12oz) daikon radish, topped, tailed and peeled
120g (4oz) golden granulated sugar
25g (1oz) sea salt flakes

For the pickling liquid
300ml (10fl oz/ 1¼ cups) water
150g (5oz/scant 1⅔ cups) golden granulated sugar
2 tsp sea salt flakes
1 tsp ground turmeric
150ml (5fl oz/scant ⅔ cup) cider vinegar

Halve the radishes so you have two half-moon-shaped batons. Cut them in half again if the radishes are too long. Arrange the radishes nice and flat in a container in which they fit snugly – a 1 litre (34fl oz/4 cup) tub is perfect – or in a resealable bag. Sprinkle the sugar and salt over the top. Cover and leave to sit at room temperature, away from the direct sun, for 3 days, turning daily to ensure the radishes are evenly saturated; radishes will naturally release a fair amount of water and shrink in size.

Discard the liquid and transfer the radishes to a suitable heatproof container with a lid (which may be the now clean container you previously used).

Make the pickling liquid by placing the water, sugar, salt and ground turmeric in a small saucepan. Whisk together to combine and bring to a gentle simmer over a low heat to dissolve the sugar. Once hot, stir in the vinegar and simmer for a minute to warm. Remove from the heat and pour the liquid over the radishes. Press down gently to ensure the radishes are submerged in the brine. Put the lid on ajar and let everything cool down a little before securing properly.

Once chilled completely, store in the fridge. The radishes will take about a week to pickle fully and develop a good flavour, at which point you can cut them into half-moon slices to serve, or use them in the salad on page 114. The pickle will keep well for about a month.

CAN'T WAIT

It pays to be patient, but if you do want to eat the pickles sooner, slice the dehydrated radishes into 5mm (¼in) thick half-moon shapes after the first 3 days, before pouring the pickling liquid. It will be ready to eat after 24 hours.

Spicy Pickled Radish Salad

Danmuji Muchim

Beautifully balanced, salty-sweet flavours of Korean pickled radish make a great canvas for fruity *gochugaru* and savoury sesame oil. A touch of vinegar brings a fresh layer of brightness and amplifies the piquant flavour. It's great to serve with any rice or noodle dishes to add a little texture and has the added benefit of being ready in minutes.

Danmuji (Korean sweet pickled radish) is typically found in the refrigerated isle in Korean supermarkets and comes in various sizes and colours, either dyed yellow or natural. Both types work fine for this recipe.

SERVES 6

400–450g (14–16oz) *danmuji* from page 110, or available in Korean supermarkets
1 garlic clove, minced
2 spring onions (scallions), minced
½ tsp golden granulated sugar
1 tsp *gochugaru* (Korean red pepper flakes)
1 tsp toasted white sesame seeds
1 tsp light or soup soy sauce
1 tsp cider vinegar
1 tbsp toasted sesame oil
sea salt flakes, to taste

Slice the *danmuji* thinly into half-moon shapes; if you are using shop-bought *danmuji* that comes whole, cut it in half lengthways first before slicing into half-moons. Transfer to a mixing bowl.

Add the rest of the ingredients, except the salt, and toss together to combine by hand, massaging firmly to distribute the seasoning evenly. Check for seasoning and adjust it with a pinch more sugar or a little salt, if you like. You can serve immediately or store in the fridge to enjoy later. It will keep well in the fridge for about a week.

White Cabbage Salad with Yogurt Dressing

Yangbaechu Salad

Asak asak is the texture and mouthfeel that Koreans focus on in this dish, teasing the fibrous strands of the raw cabbage into something pleasingly crunchy. The creamy yogurt-based dressing is sweetened just enough to sing, and the neutral, almost bland taste of the cabbage transforms to show off its natural sweetness, bringing the joy of plain and simple deliciousness. My love for this humble brassica is infinite and unconditional. I can quite happily eat many platefuls in one sitting.

This makes about 180ml (6fl oz/¾ cup) of dressing, which should be plenty to dress the salad with some left over.

SERVES 2–4

¼ white cabbage

For the dressing
100g (3½oz) Greek yogurt
40g (1½oz) mayonnaise
30g (1oz) onion,
   roughly chopped
1 tbsp chopped
   pickled gherkins
1½ tsp golden granulated
   sugar
juice of ½ lemon
sea salt flakes, to taste
freshly cracked black
   pepper, to taste

Prepare the cabbage by removing the core and any wilted outer leaves. Using a sharp knife, mandoline or vegetable peeler, slice the cabbage into very fine strands. Transfer the shredded cabbage to a large mixing bowl and soak in cold water for 10 minutes. Drain well and set aside.

Meanwhile, make the dressing by combining the yogurt, mayonnaise, onion, gherkins, sugar and lemon juice in a food processor. Blend until smooth. You may want to loosen with a touch of water; for me this is about 1 teaspoon. Season generously with a pinch of salt and plenty of black pepper. Add a pinch more sugar to taste, if desired.

Dress the cabbage generously with the yogurt dressing just before serving. You may not need all the dressing; any leftover dressing will keep well in the fridge for about 3 days.

Crudités +
Ssamjang Mayo

Jecheol Chaeso
+ Mayo Ssamjang

I can't think of any better way to showcase the generous nature of Korean hospitality than a complementary plate of cucumber and carrot sticks casually popped on the table with a bowl of *ssamjang* – a gesture we call 'service' to thank you for your custom. An unexpected plate of small *anju* dishes or a bottle of soft drinks sometimes appear as you build a good rapport with the owners. In any case, accept it with a smile, enjoy it, and spend enough to show your gratitude.

SERVES 4–6

500g (1lb 2oz) mixed seasonal vegetables (try baby carrot, radish, cucumber, celery, bitter leaves, sugar snap peas; anything crunchy and dip-able)

For the ssamjang mayo
2 tbsp mayonnaise
2 tbsp *doenjang* (Korean fermented bean paste)
1 tbsp *gochujang* (Korean fermented chilli paste)
1 tbsp rice vinegar
1 tbsp toasted sesame oil
1 tsp golden granulated sugar
1 tsp *gochugaru* (Korean red pepper flakes)
1 tsp toasted white sesame seeds
2 garlic cloves, minced
1 spring onion (scallion), minced

Make the *ssamjang* mayo at least one day in advance by combining all the ingredients in an airtight container and refrigerating it. When the sauce is left to mature, the sharp edges of raw ingredients start to soften to bring a more rounded overall flavour.

Place the vegetables on a platter in a visually pleasing way. Think of arranging a beautiful bouquet of vegetables to show off seasonality, colour and texture, leaving a little gap on the plate for the *ssamjang* mayo. It can be as simple or as elaborate as you like. Transfer the *ssamjang* mayo to a bowl and serve alongside the vegetables for dipping.

Cucumber + Seaweed Salad

Oi Miyeok Cho Muchim

The naturally salty and briny taste of seaweed complements the juicy cucumber, and brings a dish that is bright and refreshing. A light touch of sweet and tart seasoning makes it a great salad for sweltering days that require piquant flavours to shake up the tired palate. And it's a perfect pairing for spicy dishes to offset chilli heat.

Miyeok, which is not dissimilar to Japanese *wakame,* can be found in Korean supermarkets, often in the same aisle where seaweed sheets are kept. It is sold dry and comes in various sizes and packets; some are pre-cut for the convenience.

SERVES 4–6

10g (¼oz) *miyeok* (Korean seaweed)
1 cucumber
½ tsp sea salt flakes
¼ onion, thinly sliced
1 tbsp rice vinegar
1 tbsp mirin
1 tsp toasted white sesame seeds, lightly crushed

For the dressing

1½ tbsp golden granulated sugar
1 tbsp rice vinegar
1 tbsp light or soup soy sauce
2 tsp fish sauce
zest of ½ lemon and 1 tbsp juice
1 garlic clove, grated
1 hot red chilli, thinly sliced

Soak the *miyeok* in plenty of cold water for 20 minutes. Dry seaweed does not look like much at all but, as it starts to rehydrate, it will soon double or triple in volume, so make sure the bowl you are using is big enough to accommodate the increase. Once softened, drain.

Meanwhile, top and tail the cucumber, then peel off the skin at intervals so that you have striped patterned cucumber. Halve the cucumber lengthways and scrape out and discard the watery seeds in the middle with a teaspoon, then slice thinly. Put the sliced cucumbers in a mixing bowl and combine with the salt. Leave to stand for 10 minutes. When ready, drain and set aside.

Soak the onion in cold water for 10 minutes to remove the harsh taste. When ready, drain and add to the drained cucumber.

Make the dressing by combining the sugar, vinegar, soy sauce, fish sauce and lemon zest and juice. Whisk well to dissolve the sugar. Stir in the garlic and chilli, and set aside.

Bring a large pan of water to the boil. Stir in the tablespoon of rice vinegar and mirin. Have a bowl of cold water ready, close by, so you can plunge the blanched seaweed immediately into the cold water. When the water is rapidly boiling, carefully drop the rehydrated seaweed into the water to blanch. After about 30 seconds, using tongs or a wire skimmer, transfer to the bowl of cold water. Drain completely, then gently squeeze the water out of the seaweed as much as you can by hand. Transfer to a chopping board and chop roughly.

Place the chopped seaweed into the mixing bowl with the dressing. Add the cucumber, onion and sesame seeds to the bowl. Massage gently to combine. Check for seasoning and adjust with a pinch more salt or sugar, if necessary.

Leave to sit for at least 15 minutes in the fridge or preferably overnight before serving, so the cucumber and seaweed can soak up the flavour. Serve cold. It will keep well for 3 days in the fridge, stored in an airtight container.

Long Green Chillies + Olives with Doenjang

Gochu Muchim

There once was a time when I couldn't understand why anyone would want to dip chillies in another spicy sauce. But in my adulthood, I've learned to understand that the marriage between peppery green chillies and deeply savoury *doenjang* is quite a beautiful thing. The addition of green olives – which is inspired by the cracked olive salad dish I enjoyed in my favourite family run Italian restaurant in Margate – brings a wonderfully briny salinity that complements the overall flavour.

You want to make this with long green chillies that are mild and juicy enough to burst with a little splash when you bite them. This makes a lovely accompaniment to grilled meat or is great as an easy *banchan* dish to serve with some plain steamed rice.

SERVES 4

¼ onion
200g (7oz) mild long green chillies (mixture of Turkish green chilli and long green chilli variety)
50g (2oz) green olives in brine
1 tbsp toasted white sesame seeds, lightly crushed
sea salt flakes, to taste

For the dressing

1 tbsp toasted sesame oil
1 tbsp *yondu* (seasoning sauce)
1 tsp cider vinegar
2 tsp *doenjang* (Korean fermented bean paste)
1 tsp *gochujang* (Korean fermented chilli paste)
1 tsp *jocheong* (rice syrup) or clear honey
1 garlic clove, minced

Whisk together all ingredients for the dressing in a large mixing bowl big enough to accommodate all the chillies. Set aside until needed.

Dice the onion into small bite-sized pieces. Transfer to a bowl and soak in cold water for 10 minutes to remove the strong taste. When ready, drain and transfer to the mixing bowl with the dressing.

Slice the chillies into small bite-sized pieces 2cm (¾in) thick and transfer to the same mixing bowl. Crack the olives by gently pushing the surface of the olives with the blade of a knife placed flat on top. It will naturally push out the stone in the middle and break the olives with uneven edges, which is exactly what we want. Transfer to the same mixing bowl.

Add the sesame seeds and toss everything together to combine, preferably by hand. Check for seasoning and add a pinch of salt or a touch more *jocheong*, if necessary.

Serve immediately or store in the fridge in an airtight container for up to 3 days.

Little Pick-Me-Ups

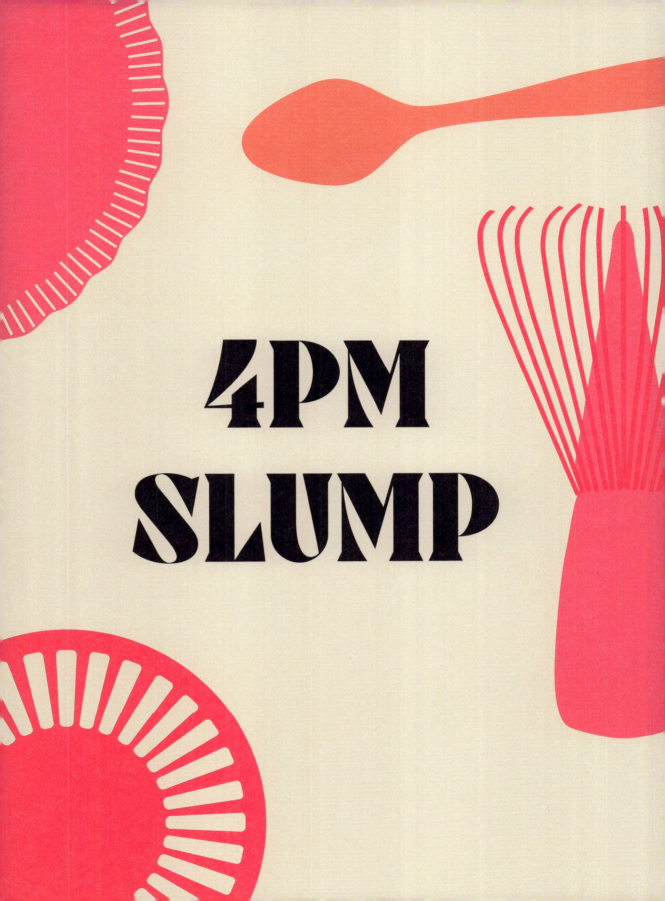

Little Pick-Me-Ups

Here's a selection of wonderful sugar-laced snacks and traditional baked goods from the streets.

Salted Nutella Pancake

Hotteok

Sweet fried pancakes are a popular street snack found in all corners of Korea all year round. They are especially sought after during the colder winter months for their delightfully crispy and chewy texture and molten hot filling.

Traditionally, wet and stretchy yeasted dough is skilfully filled with sweet cinnamon-spiced sugar and nuts, then fried in oil until the sugar turns deliciously syrupy. The dough used here is slightly drier than the traditional version, to make it easier to handle at home, though it is still high in moisture. Initially, you may find it tricky to shape the pancakes, as the dough can be quite sticky and unruly, but it does not need to be perfect so just go along with the process. A well-greased pair of hands are your best friend here. Be sure to seal the seams tightly by pressing and pinching the dough so the filling is securely encased. It does take a bit of practice but you will soon get the hang of it.

MAKES EIGHT 9CM (3½IN) PANCAKES

For the dough
180ml (6fl oz/¾ cup) warm water
2 tbsp golden caster (superfine) sugar
½ tsp fine sea salt
1 tbsp vegetable oil, plus extra for greasing and frying
150g (5oz/scant 1¼ cups) strong white bread flour
100g (3½oz/heaped ½ cup) glutinous rice flour
1 tsp fast active yeast (quick yeast)

For the filling
80g (3oz) Nutella
40g (1½oz/heaped ¼ cup) roasted peanuts, finely chopped
½ tsp sea salt flakes

Whisk together the water, sugar and salt to dissolve. Stir in the tablespoon of vegetable oil: don't worry if it doesn't incorporate well.

Meanwhile, combine both flours and the yeast in a mixing bowl. Slowly pour in the warm water and sugar mixture. Stir to combine using a wooden spoon to form a rough dough. Tip it out on a work surface and continue to work the dough to build strong gluten bonds until it becomes smooth and supple – it should take about 15 minutes; or less time if you use a stand mixer. The dough will feel quite tacky and that is perfectly okay. Wipe out, then oil the bowl. Shape the dough into a large ball and transfer to the bowl. Cover with clingfilm (plastic wrap) and rest it in a warm place for 1–1½ hours until doubled in volume.

Meanwhile, combine the filling ingredients in a small bowl and set aside. Have a large baking tray ready, lightly greased with some vegetable oil.

Once the dough has risen, rub some vegetable oil on your hands so the dough doesn't stick. Transfer the dough onto a lightly oiled surface and divide it into 8 equal dough balls, then cover.

Working with one ball at a time, gently press the dough ball flat to form a roughly palm-sized round disc. Remember, the shape doesn't need to be perfect. Put one heaped teaspoonful of the filling in the middle and gather the edges together to seal tightly at the centre, maintaining a more or less round shape. At this stage, the pancake will still resemble a dough ball. Place it seam-side down onto the oiled tray. Repeat with the rest of the dough.

Prepare a cooling rack set over a roasting tray. Place a frying pan (skillet) over a medium heat and fill generously with vegetable oil to about 1cm (½in) deep. Have a flat-based heatproof jug or spatula well-oiled and ready nearby.

Carefully transfer the shaped dough balls into the pan, a few at a time, seam-side down, and cook for 30 seconds. Flip the pancakes and press gently to flatten them with the base of the oiled jug or spatula you prepared earlier, then flip and press again to firmly seal the seam side. Fry gently for 2 minutes on each side until golden. If they brown too quickly, lower the heat slightly. Transfer to the cooling rack and continue until you have cooked all the pancakes.

The pancakes are best enjoyed warm, either on their own or with a scoop of vanilla ice cream on the side.

Candied
Sweet Potato

Mattang

For as long as I can remember, despite not having a very sweet tooth, I have always loved this sweet potato snack. Lacquered in glass-like sugar syrup, the unevenly shaped, deep-fried sweet potato eats with a satisfying crunch that swiftly transforms to fill the mouth with beautifully sticky, chewy softness. It is intensely sweet while still managing to maintain a savoury edge.

It is preferable to use a deep reddish-purple-skinned variety with paler flesh, which tend to be sweeter and nuttier and less watery than the more common orange variety, but you'll still enjoy it if you can only get the orange ones.

SERVES 2–4

350g (12oz) sweet potatoes
vegetable oil, for frying
1 tsp toasted black
  sesame seeds
sea salt flakes, to taste

For the glaze

2 tbsp golden caster
  (superfine) sugar
2 tbsp vegetable oil
2 tbsp *jocheong* (rice syrup)
  or clear honey

Peel the sweet potatoes, if preferred. Top and tail them and cut them in half lengthways. Cut each half into bite-sized chunks. Transfer to a large mixing bowl and soak in cold water for 30 minutes to remove any excess starch. Once done, drain and pat dry with a dish towel.

Set a cooling rack over a roasting tray, and lightly grease a baking tray.

Fill a large, heavy-based saucepan with enough vegetable oil to submerge the sweet potatoes but come no more than three-quarters of the way up the pan. Ensure there's plenty of space left in the pan, as when you fry the sweet potatoes, the oil will bubble and initially rise. Heat the oil to 170°C (340°F). Gently lower a few of the sweet potatoes into the oil and fry for 6 minutes until they are golden on all sides. Use a slotted spoon to transfer them to the cooling rack while you cook the remaining potatoes.

Put the glaze ingredients in a large sauté pan. Swirl the pan around a little so the sugar is saturated in oil. Bring to a simmer over a low–medium heat without disturbing the pan too much for 2–3 minutes until the glaze turns golden, almost light toffee in colour, and syrupy. Toss in the fried sweet potatoes and sesame seeds and continue cooking for 1–2 minutes, turning to coat them evenly with the glaze, until very glossy. Transfer to the greased baking tray. Sprinkle with a pinch of salt and leave to cool so the sugar sets before tucking in.

Honey Cookies

Yakgwa

Traditionally, these sweet, syrup-soaked cookies are made by pushing the dough firmly into a special *yakgwa* mould, which creates its signature flower-like patterned shape. They are then deep-fried and soaked in *jocheong* (traditional Korean rice syrup) while warm, so the sweet cinnamon-laced syrup can saturate the dough. The result is heavenly, with a texture that offers both crunchy and soft with just enough sweetness.

Once enjoyed only on special occasions – because honey used to be so expensive and therefore precious – *yakgwa* has become increasingly popular in recent years, with growing interest in the preservation of traditional sweet treats, especially when using time-honoured artisanal skills. It isn't difficult to spot many market stalls, supermarkets and cafés selling both old-fashioned and fancifully modern iterations of honey cookies that showcase the ever-evolving visions of an imaginative nation. They truly are a delicious little treat. *Pictured overleaf.*

**MAKES AROUND
32 COOKIES**

vegetable oil, for frying

For the cookie dough
200g (7oz/scant 1⅔ cups)
   plain (all-purpose) flour,
   plus extra for dusting
50g (2oz/heaped ¼ cup)
   glutinous rice flour
½ tsp ground ginger
½ tsp ground cinnamon
½ tsp fine sea salt
½ tsp freshly ground
   black pepper
2 tbsp toasted sesame oil
2 tbsp vegetable oil
60g (2oz) raw runny honey
4 tbsp sake

For the soaking syrup
200g (7oz) *jocheong*
   (rice syrup)
100ml (3½fl oz/scant
   ½ cup) water
2 tsp sliced root ginger
3cm (1¼in) cinnamon stick
sea salt flakes, to taste

Sift both flours, the ground ginger and cinnamon into a large mixing bowl. Add the salt and black pepper. Gradually stir in both the oils using a wooden spoon or chopsticks. Rub the mixture by hand to evenly blend the oils into the flour mixture until you end up with sandy crumbs.

Add the honey and sake to the mix and start bringing the dough together by gently folding the mixture with a wooden spoon or rubber spatula, scraping any dry bits to mix in with the wet. The aim isn't to build gluten bonds so do not knead the dough, instead aim to create a dough by folding and pushing the mixture. The dough may feel dry but that's perfectly okay; you can add a touch of water if you find it difficult. Transfer the dough to a reusable plastic bag or wrap with clingfilm (plastic wrap). Rest for 30 minutes in the fridge.

Meanwhile, to make the soaking syrup, put the *jocheong*, water, ginger and cinnamon in a small saucepan, place over a medium heat and whisk gently to combine. Bring to a simmer over a medium heat, then lower the heat and simmer for 6–8 minutes until it reaches a syrupy consistency that coats the back of the spoon. Remove from the heat, add a pinch of salt to taste, and leave to cool.

Transfer the dough to a sturdy work surface and start rolling it out into a sheet about 1cm (½in) thick, measuring about 10×20cm (4×8in). Smooth out the edges with a scraper. Cut the sheet in half and stack them together, then roll them out to the same size again. Repeat the cutting in half and rolling twice more to build layers within the dough, ending up with a sheet with the above measurements.

Using a sharp knife or a small cookie cutter, cut the rolled-out dough into 2.5cm (1in) squares. Make a few holes in the middle of each cookie with a fork or metal skewer.

Prepare a cooling rack set over a roasting tray.

Fill a large, heavy-based saucepan with enough vegetable oil to submerge the cookies but come no more than three-quarters of the way up the pan. Heat to 110–120°C (230–250°F) and fry the cookies in small batches for 5 minutes until they turn light golden in colour. You should notice the layers forming as the cookies fry at a low temperature. Lift out with a slotted spoon and transfer to the cooling rack.

Increase the temperature of the frying oil to 150°C (300°F). Carefully lower a few of the fried cookies into the oil and fry for 6 minutes, or until deeply woody-brown. Transfer to the cooling rack and continue with the rest of the cookies.

Transfer the warm double-fried cookies to a heatproof container. Pour the cooled syrup over the warm cookies. Cover and leave to soak at room temperature overnight, turning halfway, if necessary, to ensure an even soak.

The following day, carefully lift out the syrup-soaked cookies and transfer to a cooling rack set over a roasting tray (discard any leftover syrup). Leave the cookies to drain for at least 30 minutes before eating and up to 6 hours to set the surface dry to the touch. Traditionally the cookies are left to dry for a couple of days before storing. Once done, transfer to a lidded container and store at room temperature for up to a couple of weeks.

Fish-Shaped Peanut Butter + Jam Pastries

Bungeoppang

The classic, sweet, red-bean-paste-filled *bungeoppang* was the first ever Korean street snack my daughter tried when she was about two. While she wasn't so sure about the red bean filling, she enjoyed the crisp fish-shaped batter that ate softly chewy and warm, like the pancakes she loved eating at home. I liked how the familiar taste and texture of something else could lend her a sense of comfort, easing her into the lesser-known part of her culture.

When I first got myself a *bungeoppang* pan to make some more with her, I couldn't stop thinking about the toasted peanut butter and jam sandwiches I used to make with my father. Maybe it was something about the special tool that reminded me of the memories, which were painted with the smell of toasting bread and the taste of warm peanut butter jelly that used to fill me with wonder. I liked how the toasted sandwich maker left a perfectly triangle-shaped indentation with slightly burnt brown edges; it used to get me all stupidly excited, snapping the sandwiches in half to pile the triangles high on the plate.

I am often curious about what my daughter will remember about her childhood and if she will remember that first taste of this pastry in the streets of Seoul. Either way, I hope she remembers the story about peanut butter jelly sandwiches and perfectly messy slow days in the kitchen, making these pastries with me.

You will need a special fish-shaped *bungeoppang* pan to make these, which you can find online.

MAKES 10 PASTRIES

vegetable oil, for greasing

For the batter
150g (5oz/scant 1¼ cups) plain (all-purpose) flour
50g (2oz/heaped ¼ cup) glutinous rice flour
2 tbsp golden caster (superfine) sugar
1 tsp bicarbonate of soda (baking soda)
1 tsp baking powder
¾ tsp fine sea salt
30g (1oz) unsalted butter, melted
1 egg, lightly whisked
150ml (5fl oz/scant ⅔ cup) full-fat milk
120ml (4fl oz/½ cup) water

For the filling
125g (4oz) peanut butter (crunchy or smooth)
40g (1½oz) strawberry jam

Combine both flours, the sugar, bicarbonate of soda, baking powder and salt in a mixing bowl. Add the butter and egg. Whisk in the milk and water to form a smooth batter. Transfer to a jug with a pouring spout, cover and refrigerate for 30 minutes to rest the batter.

Mix together the peanut butter and jam in a small bowl.

When ready to make the pastries, prepare a cooling rack set over a roasting tray and lightly grease the inside of the *bungeoppang* pan with vegetable oil. Preheat the pan over a low–medium heat. When the pan has warmed up nicely, carefully pour the batter into each mould to fill about halfway. Spoon about 2 teaspoons of the peanut butter and jam filling in the middle, then top with more batter to cover the filling.

Securely close the *bungeoppang* pan. Turn the pan over immediately and cook for 3 minutes. Then flip the pan again and cook on the other side for 2 minutes. Flip the pan over briefly (about 30 seconds) once more to ensure the batter is cooked through, golden and crisp – check them and cook for a little longer if needed. When done, transfer to the cooling rack and leave to cool until just warm, before serving while you cook the remaining batter.

Salted Soy Sauce Caramel Bites

Ganjang Caramel

One of the things I always try to hunt down whenever I visit Korea are these beautifully packaged milk caramel bites. Often found in convenience stores, these perfectly bite-sized squared caramels come individually wrapped in silver foiled paper; they are a classic confectionery, loved by all for their milky toffee-like taste and softly chewy texture.

A few years ago, I came across another caramel that was seasoned with soy sauce. It gave the caramel a depth of umami salinity that was subtly detectable. I always like to add a sprinkle of salt to my sweet things, as I feel it balances and accentuates the sweetness, the same way that I think sugar can make things taste more savoury. The soy sauce and salt used here layer different kinds of salty flavour, which I think is rather nice.

MAKES ONE 10×15CM (4×6IN) SLAB

a little vegetable oil,
  for greasing
150ml (5fl oz/scant ⅔ cup)
  double (heavy) cream
50ml (2fl oz/generous
  3 tbsp) milk
2 tsp soy sauce
1 tsp vanilla bean paste
125g (4oz/⅔ cup) light
  soft brown sugar
55g (2oz) *jocheong*
  (rice syrup)
1 tbsp water
1 tbsp lemon juice
25g (1oz) unsalted butter
sea salt flakes, to finish

Line a 10×15cm (4×6in) baking tray or container with parchment paper and lightly grease it with vegetable oil.

Put the double cream, milk, soy sauce and vanilla bean paste in a small saucepan. Place the pan over a low heat to gently warm the mixture, making sure it doesn't boil.

Put the sugar, *jocheong*, water and lemon juice into a heavy-based saucepan and swirl the pan around a little so the sugar is saturated in liquid. Bring to a simmer over a medium heat without disturbing the pan too much, then simmer for 5–7 minutes until the sugar has turned golden brown in colour and reached 125°C (257°F).

Carefully stir in the warm cream and milk mixture. Simmer steadily over a low heat for about 20 minutes to caramelize the mixture, stirring frequently to stop the mixture from sticking to the bottom of the pan. You should notice small bubbles erupting as it thickens. The colour should have darkened to a shade of butterscotch and the temperature should be 125°C (257°F). You can also check it is ready by dropping a small amount of mixture into a bowl of cold water. If it holds its shape firmly and doesn't make the water murky, it's done.

Stir in the butter to incorporate, then remove from the heat.

Carefully pour the caramel into the prepared tray. Wiggle the tray a little to help it spread. Sprinkle the top with a good pinch of salt. Leave to cool slightly, then transfer to the fridge to set for 4–6 hours. When done, remove from the fridge and slice the caramel with a sharp knife into 2cm (¾in) squares.

Once cut, you can wrap them individually in parchment paper, if you wish. Store them in the fridge, in an airtight container lined with lightly greased paper to keep them separated.

Canned Peach + Ginger Beer Sorbet

Hwangdo

Canned peaches served over ice in a manner of fruit cocktail seem to be a popular choice of sweet dish that accompanies alcoholic beverages in many pocha joints. Often served topped with an effervescent soft drink, I suspect that the refreshing taste of peach and its juice act more like a buffer to sweeten the taste of alcohol. Saccharine-sweet canned peaches straight out of the can is a taste I remember very fondly as a child growing up in Korea. Eaten fridge cold after school as a little pick-me-up treat, I appreciated the convenience of juicy soft fruit that needn't be stoned or peeled.

Inspired by these memories, I made a simple sorbet using spicy ginger beer to lift the flavour of the peaches to sit zingy on the palate. It isn't overly sweet, which I like; my daughter says it's a bit like spicy slushy in her mouth.

MAKES ENOUGH TO FILL A 1 LITRE (34FL OZ/ 4 CUP) CONTAINER

415g (14oz) can of peach halves in juice
100g (3½oz) *jocheong* (rice syrup)
500ml (17fl oz/10 cups) non-alcoholic ginger beer
50ml (generous 3 tbsp) fresh lime juice

Set a sieve over a small saucepan, drain the canned peach halves and collect the juice in the pan. Add the *jocheong* to the pan and slowly warm the mixture over a low heat, stirring to combine. Once the juice and *jocheong* are fully incorporated, remove the pan from the heat and leave to cool slightly.

Put the peach halves and the cooled, sweetened juice into a high-speed blender. Add half the ginger beer and all the lime juice. Blend until smooth, then stir in the remaining ginger beer.

Pour the sorbet mixture into a freezer-safe container or resealable bag. Transfer to the freezer and leave until frozen, then leave to sit at room temperature for a few minutes to loosen the mixture from the container. Cut into large chunks and transfer to the high-speed blender. Blend until smooth again to break up the ice crystals. The bright orange colour should turn almost a soft creamy yellow. Once blended smooth again, transfer to the container and store in the freezer to set before serving.

A NOTE ON BLENDING

If you don't have a high-speed blender, you can take the mixture to almost frozen, then energetically break up the ice with a fork every 30–45 minutes or so, a few times on repeat, to achieve a fairly smooth granita.

Matcha Affogato

Matcha Ice Cream

When I was grown up enough to make a fuss about going to the pub and eating lovely two- or three-course meals with a few glasses of deliciously quaffable wine, I would often end a meal with affogato. I like the intensely hot, bitter coffee that trickles down to melt the sweet, cold ice cream. The extreme opposite ends of both flavour and temperature were a magical combination and brought a feeling of sophistication that would make me feel, well, very grown up.

When I visited Seoul a few years back, I tried what was described as matcha ice cream, which came with velvety smooth, soft-serve milk ice cream layered with a verdant green matcha. The weather was intensely hot and the air was so humid to the level that sweat dripped down your forehead as soon as you stepped outside. It was uncomfortable, and we barely managed to do anything much other than strolling through the underground shopping malls and air-conditioned department stores, making frequent stops to cool down with the various ice creams and cold beverages the city has to offer. The contrast between the sweet, creamy slushy-like milk ice cream and bitterness of matcha immediately reminded me of affogato. And in that moment, there was a real sense of bliss, with time around me stopping momentarily so I could appreciate the cooling sensation. Since then, I always whip this up when something sweet and cold is needed to quench hot days.

This is, of course, by no means a recipe, rather a little treat that I think you might like. Sometimes it's just the way of life that allows me to take a moment to notice the small things I'd like to share. I hope you enjoy.

MAKES 1 SERVING

2 tsp matcha powder
2 tbsp just-boiled water
2 scoops of best vanilla
   ice cream
a pinch of sea salt,
   to taste

Put the matcha powder and water in a small cup or a jug with a pourable spout and whisk until smooth. Put the first scoop of ice cream into one of your favourite glasses or bowls and squash it down a little so it sits unevenly in the glass. Place the second scoop on top. Pour the shot of matcha gently over and around the edges of the ice cream, then sprinkle with a pinch of flaky salt.

Take yourself and the affogato to your favourite seat. Put your feet up and allow yourself the moment to enjoy this simple pleasure.

Anju – Mix + Match Bar Snacks

Hangover Cure Soups

FEASTING UNDER THE STARS

Seoul comes to life at night with a completely different vibe. People loosen their ties and the tension falls from their shoulders. The feeling of excitement rises as the city's neon lights twinkle their rainbow-coloured faces to engage with the frenzy of the crowd. The air is filled with flaming charcoal smoke, and the sweet scent of sizzling grills is noticeable in every corner of the streets. It's not difficult to feel hungry with all the mouthwatering smells tickling your nose. The following pages slip into the evening of Seoul's food scene, centred around the culture of pocha.

Anju – Mix + Match Bar Snacks

These fun small plates are often enjoyed with an alcoholic beverage: think Italian cicchetti, Spanish tapas or Catalan pinchos!

Spam + Perilla Fritters with Pickled Chilli Dipping Sauce

Spam Kkaetnip Jeon

Spam was first introduced into Korea during the Korean War of the early 1950s and used to be considered a high-value item only available via the American army. The scarcity of food supplies during and after the Korean war meant Spam was a necessity from a far-flung land that nursed the hungry nation, much as it did the soldiers and civilians during World War II.

Fast forward a few decades, with the rapid development of the meat industry in Korea and relaxed policy on imported processed meat products in the late 1980s, Spam established itself firmly in the Korean market with the help of clever marketing that inspired an image that was both premium and affordable. Even with the continuing growth of wealth and abundance of food supplies, to many Koreans, Spam still sits comfortably on the shelves as a tasty and convenient ingredient.

Often regarded as a poor-quality meat in the West, there is a certain stigma and prejudice associated with Spam and I suspect the conversation around it is likely to spark a bit of a divide in the room! But I hope that by appreciating the history of how Spam established its place on the tables of Korean homes, it will help us to have an open mind, and to try this distinctive part of Korean food culture without judgement. So, if you're up for it, these salty-sweet fritters paired with a pickled chilli dressing scream for plain steamed rice and some cold beers. Enjoy. *Pictured overleaf.*

MAKES 12–15

For the pickled chilli dipping sauce
1–2 hot red chillies, sliced
2 tbsp water
1 tbsp golden granulated sugar
¼ tsp sea salt flakes
1 tbsp cider vinegar

For the fritters
1 egg
1 tsp oyster sauce
¼ tsp freshly cracked black pepper
4 spring onions (scallions), finely chopped
1 hot green chilli, finely chopped
200g (7oz) canned Spam

For the stuffed perilla leaves
2 tbsp plain (all-purpose) flour, for dusting
12–15 perilla leaves
2 eggs
sea salt flakes
vegetable oil, for frying

To make the chilli dipping sauce, put the chillies in a small heatproof bowl. Combine the water, sugar and salt in a small saucepan and heat gently to dissolve the sugar. Stir in the vinegar, then pour over the chillies. Set aside to cool.

To make the fritters, crack the egg into a large mixing bowl and whisk lightly. Stir in the oyster sauce, black pepper, spring onions and chilli. Rinse the Spam with just-boiled water to remove some oil, then pat it dry with kitchen paper. Coarsely grate into the mixing bowl with the egg and stir well to combine.

Put the flour in a tray or shallow, rimmed bowl. Have the bowl with the Spam mixture ready and another tray or plate close by so you can transfer the stuffed perilla leaves as you go along.

Lightly coat the underside (less green-looking side) of the perilla leaves with flour. Lay the perilla leaves flat onto a clean surface, floured-side up. Spread about 1–1½ tablespoons of the Spam mixture onto the right side of the centre seam, leaving a little space around the edges. Fold to cover and gently press to seal. Transfer to the tray or plate. Repeat with the remaining leaves and filling.

Whisk the two eggs in a bowl with a pinch of salt.

Set up your working station, as you will be dredging and frying at the same time. You need a row of the stuffed perilla leaves, the tray or bowl with the remaining flour, the whisked eggs, a frying pan (skillet) and a tray or plate lined with kitchen paper so that you can swiftly transfer the cooked fritters.

Heat about 2 tablespoons of vegetable oil in a frying pan (skillet) over a medium heat. Lightly dust a stuffed perilla leaf in flour; I like to dust only on one side to keep the vibrant green on the other side. Dip the dusted stuffed perilla leaf in the egg, ensuring it is coated evenly, then place in the frying pan. Fry it for a couple of minutes on each side until deliciously golden. Dust, dip and fry all the stuffed leaves, working in batches.

Serve warm with the pickled chilli dipping sauce on the side.

FIRST COME, FIRST TURNED

If you are cooking anything like these fritters where you are adding and removing things from the pan, there's an easy way to remember which is ready to turn or remove next. Imagine your pan is a clock face – put the first fritter in at one o'clock, then work your way clockwise round the pan. You can then just keep moving clockwise, turning and removing as they are ready.

Corn Cheese with Green Chilli + Lime

Corn Cheese

I used to frequent a small Japanese-style restaurant in a buzzing neighbourhood of Hongik University known as Hongdae, in which they sold a dish of buttered corn cooked on a hot plate topped with an egg and mysterious green sprinkles. The buttered corn I enjoyed at the time didn't have any cheese melted on top, but instead, it was enriched with an oozing golden egg yolk. I think there may have been a bit of crisp green pepper that added some contrasting texture. Since then, I have learned that the non-identifiable green sprinkles on top were dried parsley, and that this dish that I loved for its simplicity was in fact an earlier incarnation of what is nowadays famously known as Korean corn cheese.

The key to this dish, for me, is to achieve crispy golden kernels by cooking the corn until it caramelizes around the edges. Savoury with a touch of sweetness, the richness of this dish is offset with zingy chilli and lime sauce. It is great on its own or serve it with some tortilla chips on the side, and definitely with some cold beers.

SERVES 4

25g (1oz) unsalted butter
1 small onion, diced
100g (3½oz) low-
  moisture mozzarella,
  coarsely grated
25g (1oz) parmesan, grated

For the chilli + lime sauce
2 jalapeño chillies,
  roughly chopped
1 garlic clove, crushed
zest of 1 fresh lime
  plus juice of ½
10g (¼oz) flat-leaf
  parsley, stalks included,
  roughly chopped
1 tsp golden granulated
  sugar
a pinch of sea salt flakes,
  to taste

For the sweetcorn
2 × 198g (7oz) cans
  of sweetcorn
2 tbsp mayonnaise
2 tsp golden granulated
  sugar
½ tsp freshly cracked
  black pepper
½ tsp sea salt flakes

Place all the ingredients for the chilli and lime sauce into a small food processor and blend until smooth and saucy; you may need to add a touch of water (about 1 tablespoon). Check for seasoning and add a pinch more salt or sugar to taste; it should have bright acidity with a touch of heat and a sweet note.

Combine the ingredients for the sweetcorn in a mixing bowl and set aside.

Place a grill-safe, heavy-based frying pan or skillet (ideally a cast-iron skillet) over a medium heat. Melt the butter and sauté the onions for 5 minutes or so until softened. Stir the sweetcorn mixture into the pan and sauté for a couple of minutes to cook off some of the moisture. Spread the sweetcorn evenly across the pan. Lower the heat and scatter with both cheeses. Continue cooking for 10 minutes over a low heat until the edges start to appear crisp and caramelized and the cheeses have softened and look quite pale.

Meanwhile, preheat the grill (broiler) to high.

Remove the pan from the heat and place it under the grill for 2–5 minutes to continue cooking until the cheeses melt to bubbling hot and deliciously golden. Once done, carefully transfer the pan to a heatproof surface. Generously dollop the chilli and lime sauce over the top and serve immediately.

Butter Grilled Squid + Horseradish Mayo

Ojingeo Gui

Often sighted in streets and in snack kiosks in cinemas, I find it really hard to walk past the buttery smell of this moreish squid snack without wanting to have some. The delicately resistant texture of squid makes each mouthful more intensely savoury as you chew; it fills the mouth with the scent of salty-sweet ocean flavours, rich and heavy on the umami. And I strongly agree with the Korean maxim that says grilled squid (of all kinds) calls for cold beers.

SERVES 1–2

200g (7oz) fresh squid, thawed if frozen
2 garlic cloves
2 hot green chillies, roughly chopped
25g (1oz) unsalted butter
1 tbsp golden granulated sugar
1 tsp light or soup soy sauce
¼ tsp freshly cracked black pepper
1 spring onion (scallion), green part thinly sliced (reserve the white part for another time)
sea salt flakes, to taste

For the horseradish mayo
1 tbsp mayonnaise
1 tsp horseradish sauce
1 small garlic clove, grated
2 tsp fresh lemon juice
½ tsp snipped chives
sea salt flakes, to taste

Combine all the ingredients for the horseradish mayo in a small mixing bowl, then set aside.

Open the squid out flat by inserting a sharp knife inside to cut along the natural line. Once flat, scrape off any membranes and rinse under running water. Pat the squid dry with kitchen paper. Score the inside of the body in a criss-cross pattern with a sharp knife, ensuring the knife is only inserted about one-third of the way into the flesh at an angle. Cut into manageable widths, then into 1.5cm (⅝in) thick rectangular strips. Cut the tentacles into similar-length pieces, if using. Repeat with the other squid, if appropriate.

Bring a pan of water to a rapid boil. Have a bowl of cold water ready close by so you can plunge the blanched squid immediately into cold water. When the water is rapidly boiling, carefully drop in the squid and blanch for 30 seconds. Using a wire skimmer, transfer the squid to the bowl of cold water, then drain thoroughly. Set aside.

Put the garlic and chillies into a mortar and pestle. Pound to a rough paste; you may use a pinch of salt as an abrasive to help with pounding.

Melt the butter in a frying pan (skillet) or wok over a medium heat until it appears golden brown and smells deliciously nutty. Swiftly add the garlic and chilli paste and stir briefly to cook out the rawness and release the flavour. Add the sugar, soy sauce, black pepper and blanched squid. Increase the heat to high and flash-fry the squid for 2 minutes or so until it is cooked through, while tossing energetically to combine. Stir in the sliced spring onion greens. Check for seasoning and add a pinch of salt, if necessary. Serve immediately with the horseradish mayo on the side.

Pan-Fried Skate + Wasabi Butter Sauce

Gajami Gui

Escaping the hustle and bustle of main strips in Namdaemun market in Seoul, which is a large traditional market known for its maze-like alleys specializing in a variety of goods, I stumbled across a quieter narrow alley famous for braised belt fish and assorted fried fish. The late morning sun was rising just about high enough to break through the gaps of crowded roofs and it lit the dim back alley, making it look beautiful and moody. I liked the way the gentle spring air so boldly carried a mouthwatering smell of frying fish, tickling my nose to excite my hungry belly.

Inspired by the belt fish alley, here I dust the fish heavily with flour, before frying it in a glug of oil until its pale white coat turns a nutty brown. The craggy crust of skate wing becomes crunchy, with its creamy flesh remaining tender and delicate. Wasabi butter sauce wasn't served with the fish in Namdaemun market, but I think it goes with the skate rather well. This is a simple one-pan dish that goes well with rice or fries.

SERVES 2

400g (14oz) skate wing
  (2 small wings or
  1 large piece to share)
sea salt flakes, to taste
plain (all-purpose) flour,
  for dusting
vegetable oil, for frying
2 cheeks of lemon,
  to serve (optional)

For the wasabi butter sauce
4 tbsp sake
4 tbsp cider vinegar
6 tbsp water
1 tbsp soy sauce
1 tbsp *yondu*
  (seasoning sauce)
1 tsp golden granulated
  sugar
40g (1½oz) cold unsalted
  butter, diced
2 tsp wasabi paste
1 tbsp snipped chives
freshly cracked black
  pepper, to taste

Pat the fish dry with kitchen paper and season generously with salt. Dust the fish generously with flour and shake off any excess. Heat a little vegetable oil in a large frying pan (skillet) over a medium heat. The oil shouldn't be screaming hot but hot enough to hear a gentle sizzle when you lay in the fish. Fry the fish for 4–5 minutes on each side until cooked through and beautifully golden and crisp. Once done, transfer to a serving plate and keep warm while you make the sauce.

Wipe down the same frying pan with kitchen paper. Add the sake, cider vinegar, water, soy sauce, *yondu* and sugar to the pan. Let it come to a gentle bubble and reduce over a low heat for about 4 minutes until there is only about one-third of the liquid left. You should notice the small bubbles gather around the side. Gradually stir in a few cubes of the butter at a time to emulsify, whisking to ensure the mixture doesn't become too hot, to prevent the sauce from splitting. The sauce should be smooth and voluminous and have the colour of dark butterscotch. Remove from the heat. Whisk in the wasabi paste and the chives, then season liberally with black pepper. Pour the sauce generously over the skate wing. Serve immediately with a cheek of lemon for squeezing over, if using.

Candied Soy Sauce Nuts

Gyeongwaryu Jorim

The combination of candied nuts seasoned with soy sauce and eaten with rice might sound strange for some, but in Korea this particular way of serving nuts is common as part of a meal. Much praised for its health benefits, thanks to the assorted combination of nuts and seeds, this trail-mix-esque dish is also loved as a simple beer snack that can be whipped up in no time. Their sweetness is delicately balanced with the umami flavours of soy sauce, making these nuts very moreish.

SERVES 2–4

3 tbsp water
1 tbsp soy sauce
2 tsp golden granulated
   sugar
1 tbsp *jocheong* (rice syrup)
   or clear honey
150g (5oz/heaped 1 cup)
   mixed nuts (walnuts,
   macadamias, peanuts,
   almonds or cashews
   all work well)
1 tbsp extra virgin olive oil
1 tsp toasted white
   sesame seeds
sea salt flakes, to taste
freshly cracked black
   pepper, to taste

Put the water, soy sauce and sugar in a small mixing bowl and stir well to dissolve the sugar. Add the *jocheong* but don't worry too much about dissolving it as it will not mix in well; it will dissolve easily once things warm up.

Heat a wok or frying pan (skillet) over a low–medium heat. Add the nuts and dry-fry for 1–2 minutes to bring out the nuttiness – much the same way you would with spices; this process will also help to remove the bitter taste that can linger from an old bag of nuts.

Add the olive oil to the pan and toss gently to coat the nuts with the oil, then fry for 1 minute. Reduce the heat a little. Stir in the soy sauce seasoning and combine well. As the sugar starts to melt, it will smell beautifully sweet with the caramelizing soy sauce scent. Continue cooking for about 3 minutes until the sauce has thickened and reduced to coat the nuts in a glossy and delicious glaze.

Remove from the heat and stir in the sesame seeds. Add a good pinch of salt and black pepper to taste. If you wish to serve the dish cold, spread the nut mixture onto a lined tray to cool before storing, so they don't clump together. Otherwise, serve while warm.

Lazy Oven Chips + Magic Savoury Salt

Gamja twigim

When developing this recipe, I was initially thinking of a seasoning that was going to be sprinkled on tornado potato – a famous Korean street food of deep-fried, twisted, spiral-cut potato my daughter adores. That then led me to think of crispy fried noodle snacks sprinkled with instant-noodle sachet seasoning called *ramyunttang* that I used to enjoy as a child. Then it got me thinking. Why not on chips? Simple potato fries topped with all manner of toppings and/ or sauces are universally popular, and easy to make at home.

So here is my recipe for lazy oven chips smothered in magic savoury salt that clings onto the hot, fatty surface and slaps all the senses of flavour: hot, sour, salty, sweet, bitter and umami. The generous use of Sichuan and white pepper laces the salt with a deliciously tongue-tingling heat, while *gochugaru* imparts a gentle fruity spiciness in the background. Balanced with a little sugar and amchoor powder (the sour spice powder of unripe green mango commonly used in Indian cooking), the dish ends with a lovely citrusy acidity.

The spice mix can be made in advance and stored in an airtight jar. It will keep well for several weeks. Delicious with fried chicken or grilled buttered corn, it's pretty versatile stuff and quite addictive.

**SERVES 4
WITH LEFTOVER
SAVOURY SALT**

4 servings of good-quality oven chips (I like thin-cut French fries)

For the savoury salt
1 tbsp Sichuan peppercorns
1 tbsp white peppercorns
1 tsp *gochugaru* (Korean red pepper flakes)
1 tbsp sea salt flakes
1 tsp golden granulated sugar
2 tsp amchoor powder (dried mango powder)

Preheat the oven and prepare the chips/fries according to the packet instructions. I like to cook mine for slightly longer than the guided instruction, turning frequently to crisp up evenly.

To make the savoury salt, put the Sichuan peppercorns and white peppercorns in a small heavy-based saucepan and dry roast for a few minutes over a low heat. Leave to cool. Transfer to a spice or coffee grinder and blend until smooth. Add the *gochugaru*, salt and sugar, and blend to a very fine powder. Stir in the amchoor powder and whizz briefly to combine. Tip the mixture into a jar and give it a good shake.

When the chips are ready, transfer to a large mixing bowl and sprinkle generously with the savoury salt mix while hot. Give them a good toss so the seasoning evenly coats the chips. Serve immediately with condiments of your choice for dipping.

Volcano Egg

Poktan Gyeran Jjim

I wrote about Korean soft steamed egg in my first book, *Rice Table*, which is set delicately with elegance, almost like panna cotta. This is a more rustic and fun version that yields fluffy soufflé-like egg, typically cooked in a traditional earthenware dish called *ttukbaegi*. The loose egg mixture is stirred lovingly until you can feel the weight of the whisked eggs gently lapping around the spoon, which tells you the eggs are ready to rise and set. Soon, gently curdled cream-like eggs start to bubble and steam, then erupt to reveal their beautifully ragged tenderness. And all in just 10 minutes.

SERVES 1–2

3 eggs, about 150g (5oz)
1 tsp mirin
1 tsp toasted sesame oil
½ tsp golden granulated
   sugar
½ tsp baking powder
½ tsp sea salt flakes
150ml (5fl oz/scant
   ⅔ cup) water
1 tsp *yondu*
   (seasoning sauce)

To finish

1 spring onion (scallion),
   green parts only,
   thinly sliced
¼ tsp toasted white
   sesame seeds
¼ tsp *gochugaru*
   (Korean red pepper
   flakes), optional

Crack the eggs into a mixing bowl and whisk energetically until very smooth. Add the mirin, sesame oil, sugar, baking powder and salt. Whisk to combine, ensuring the sugar and salt have completely dissolved.

Put the water and *yondu* into a *ttukbaegi*, if you have one; a small clay pot with a lid will also work okay. Bring the water to a rapid boil.

Reduce the heat to medium so the water stays at a high simmer. Pour the egg mixture into the water. You want the water and egg mixture to come up to fill around 80 per cent of the pot height, leaving a little space on top for it to rise. Start stirring in one direction, scraping the bottom of the pot to ensure it doesn't burn at the bottom. Notice after about 2 minutes that the mixture starts to feel more weighty and looks almost curdled. At this point, lower the heat immediately and scatter the top with the spring onion, sesame seeds and *gochugaru*, if using. Cover the pot with another upturned pan or a heatproof bowl to create a lid that leaves room for the eggs to rise as they steam; I use a 6cm (2½in) deep bowl.

Cook for 2 minutes over a low heat, then turn off the heat and let it sit for another 30 seconds to steam in the residual heat.

Carefully lift the lid off and place the pan onto a heatproof surface so you can serve immediately while warm. Spoon out soft mounds and serve with rice.

TTUKBAEGI

This traditional earthenware dish is really good at retaining heat and brilliant for making stews, one-pot rice dishes and many more recipes. They are not too expensive and you can find them in all sorts of different sizes in large Korean supermarkets or online. For this recipe, you will need a *ttukbaegi* with a 9cm (3½in) diameter base (12cm/4½in wide at the top) that comfortably fits 450ml (15¾fl oz/scant 2 cups) of liquid.

Potato, Chive +
Gruyère Pancake

Cheese Gamja Jeon

I always think there are more connections and similarities in food and culture across the continents than we sometimes think. Take this Korean potato pancake, for example, often made with grated potato, a common element of a good rösti or German potato pancake, or Jewish latkes (which are derived from an Italian dish). That commonality brings a comforting familiarity.

I prefer to peel the potatoes for this recipe but if the variety you are using has a thin skin, you can scrub the potatoes and leave the skin on. Coarsely grated potatoes yield a texture that is perfectly tender and crispy to bite into. The gentle flavour of soft chive mingles delicately among the nuttiness of melting and caramelizing Gruyère cheese. It pairs perfectly with cold drinks – especially delicious with *makgeolli* or beer – and makes a great lunch to tide the peckish belly over to dinner, or a snack to entertain the chilled vibes of a slow, rainy afternoon.

**MAKES ABOUT
18 PANCAKES**

600g (1lb 5oz) floury
   potatoes, such as
   Maris Piper, Russet
   or Yukon Gold
sea salt flakes, to taste
1 onion, coarsely grated
2 tbsp rice flour
100g (3½oz) Gruyère,
   coarsely grated
3 tbsp snipped chives
½ tsp freshly cracked
   black pepper
vegetable oil, for frying

For the dipping sauce
1 tbsp soy sauce
1 tbsp rice vinegar
1 tbsp water
1 tsp golden granulated
   sugar
1 red bird's eye
   chilli, chopped

Make the dipping sauce by combining all the sauce ingredients in a small mixing bowl. Set aside.

Prepare the potatoes by carefully grating them by hand using the coarse side of a box grater, making sure the grater is resting securely on a sturdy surface. I like to rest it over a mixing bowl so the grated potatoes fall straight into the bowl. Add a good pinch of salt and combine well.

Take a handful of grated potato, hold your hand over the bowl and squeeze to wring out as much liquid as possible, then put the squeezed potatoes into a large, clean mixing bowl. Continue until all the potatoes are in the clean bowl.

Leave the bowl with the juices to stand for 10 minutes undisturbed so that the starch separates from the liquid, which will pool to the bottom of the bowl. Carefully pour away and discard the liquid on top, then pour the remaining white starch into the potatoes. Add the onion, rice flour, Gruyère, chives and black pepper. Stir in about ½ teaspoon of sea salt flakes, or to taste, and mix thoroughly to combine.

Have a tray or plate lined with kitchen paper ready so you can swiftly transfer the cooked pancakes.

Heat about 2 tablespoons of vegetable oil in a large frying pan (skillet) over a low–medium heat. The oil should be warm enough to crisp up the pancakes but not smoking. When the oil has warmed up nicely, carefully ladle the batter into the pan – you should hear a sizzling sound when the batter hits the oil. Spread the batter to make a palm-sized pancake measuring about 5mm (¼in) thick and 6cm (2½in) in diameter and cook for 2–3 minutes. You will notice the edge of the pancake starting to crisp up, the batter setting to hold everything together and the bottom browning nicely. You should also smell the cheese caramelizing. You may need to add a touch more oil occasionally around the edge of the pan as you go.

Carefully flip the pancake over and press the middle gently to help the ingredients settle. Cook for a further 2 minutes, or until cooked through and golden, then transfer to the prepared tray or plate. Continue working through the rest of batter, adding a little more vegetable oil from time to time. Serve immediately while warm with the dipping sauce on the side. The pancakes are also great served cold, although they do lose their crisp texture.

Kimchi Pancake

Kimchi Buchimgae / Kimchi Jeon

As with all simple cooking, I think making a good kimchi pancake relies on a few basic fundamentals: a flavoursome kimchi that is ripe enough to carry some tanginess, with decent bite that's not too mushy or soft; and a good temperature and oil control to achieve an overall texture that retains crispiness with a contrastingly tender and squishy middle. The sourness of overripe kimchi should be balanced with a touch of sugar and the batter should be seasoned appropriately – accordingly to the kimchi you're using – to taste savoury and moreish.

I am also of the opinion that the joys of eating pancakes can be found in the tearing and sharing; a friendly fight that involves gnarly and rustic manoeuvres of chopsticks. We pull and break apart the freshly fried golden pancakes to polish off in togetherness, from the crispiest edges to the last tender crumb. Dip patiently, to let the pancake soak up the gentle acidity of the salty-sweet vinegary sauce, which cuts through the fat. It is a sociable snack that pairs well with cold beers and a good chinwag.

MAKES ABOUT 4 PANCAKES

250g (9oz) very ripe cabbage kimchi, drained and roughly chopped
½ onion, sliced
vegetable oil, for frying

For the batter
150g (5oz/scant 1¼ cups) plain (all-purpose) flour
3 tbsp rice flour
1 tsp golden granulated sugar
1 tsp *gochugaru* (Korean red pepper flakes)
½ tsp baking powder
½ tsp sea salt flakes
¼ tsp ground white pepper
1 tbsp toasted sesame oil
280ml (9fl oz/generous 1 cup) fridge-cold water

For the dipping sauce
2 tbsp rice vinegar
1 tbsp soy sauce
1 tbsp water
1 tsp golden granulated sugar
½ tsp *gochugaru* (Korean red pepper flakes)
1 hot green chilli, chopped

Place all the dry ingredients for the batter in a large mixing bowl and give them a brief stir before adding the sesame oil and cold water. Whisk roughly – using chopsticks or a wooden spoon – to break up any lumps, then chill to rest the batter for 30 minutes or overnight, if you prefer. The batter will thicken slightly as the flour swells while it is resting.

Meanwhile make the dipping sauce by combining all the sauce ingredients in a small mixing bowl.

Add the chopped kimchi and onion to the rested batter. Give it a good stir to combine well.

Heat about 2 tablespoons of vegetable oil in a large frying pan (skillet) over a medium heat. The oil should be warm enough to crisp up the pancakes but not smoking. Carefully ladle the batter into the middle of the pan – you should hear a sizzling sound when the batter hits the oil. Spread the batter to make a pancake about 5–10mm (¼–½in) thick and 20cm (8in) in diameter. Soon, you will notice the edge of the pancake starting to crisp up. Gently swirl the pan to move the oil in and around the pancake, so the oil can reach the bottom of the pancake. You may need to add a touch more oil as you go, if the pan appears or sounds a little dry.

After about 3 minutes, you will notice dry patches on the top of the pancake that indicate that the batter is almost cooked. Drizzle a little more vegetable oil on top then carefully flip the pancake over. Press the centre gently to help the ingredients settle. Cook for a further 2 minutes, or until cooked through and golden. Continue working through the rest of the batter.

Serve immediately with the dipping sauce on the side. Leftover pancakes can be stored in the fridge and brought to room temperature before being reheated in a hot pan with a little oil to crisp them up again.

Braised Ham Hock

Jokbal

A platter of beautifully glossy, caramel-coloured slices of boiled hock is what I would call a dish fit for all manner of special occasions. It is a dish that celebrates the incredible layer of melt-in-your-mouth fat that sits atop this flavourful meat. The gelatinous skin carries the most wonderful aromas of sweet spices and its bouncy texture is much treasured among fans of this classic dish. It certainly isn't for the faint-hearted.

The dish is more commonly served with a salted, fermented shrimp-based sauce, called *saeujeot*, which you can often find in the freezer section of Korean supermarkets. My sauce is adapted using fish sauce, which is more widely available.

SERVES 4

1 unsmoked ham hock,
   up to 1.5kg (3lb 5oz)
½ tsp toasted sesame oil
toasted white sesame seeds

For the braising liquid
125g (4oz/⅔ cup) light soft
   brown sugar
120ml (4fl oz/½ cup) soy sauce
120ml (4fl oz/½ cup)
   soju or sake
3 tbsp blackstrap molasses
3 tbsp *jocheong* (rice syrup)
   or clear honey
5 spring onions (scallions),
   roots attached
1 onion, halved with skin
   left on
1 sweet apple (or Asian
   pear), halved and cored
   with skin left on
30g (1oz) garlic cloves,
   peeled and kept whole
20g (¾oz) root ginger, sliced
3 dried red chillies
3 star anise
2 dried bay leaves
1 tbsp black peppercorns
2 litres (70fl oz/8 cups) water
1 cinnamon stick, about
   5cm (2in) long
sea salt flakes, to taste

For the dipping sauce
1 tbsp fish sauce
1 tbsp rice vinegar
2 tbsp water
1 tbsp golden granulated sugar
½ tsp *gochugaru* (Korean
   red pepper flakes)
½ tsp toasted white sesame
   seeds, lightly crushed
¼ tsp freshly cracked
   black pepper
1 garlic clove, minced
1 hot green or red
   chilli, minced

Pat the ham hock dry with kitchen paper to remove the sitting blood, if any. If you spot any hair on the skin, remove it with a sharp razor or blow torch.

Put the ham hock into a large saucepan and fill with enough just-boiled water to submerge the meat. Bring to the boil with the lid on, then remove the lid and boil rapidly for 8–10 minutes. You should notice scum gathering around the edges of the pan. Remove from the heat and drain carefully, then rinse thoroughly to remove any scum stuck around the bone. Set aside.

Clean the stockpot and prepare the braising liquid. Put the sugar, soy sauce, soju (or sake), blackstrap molasses and *jocheong* in the stockpot. Add all the remaining ingredients for the braising liquid except the cinnamon stick and salt. Put on the lid, bring to the boil, then simmer for 15 minutes over a medium heat.

Carefully submerge the ham hock in the braising liquid and add the cinnamon stick. Cover with the lid ajar and simmer steadily for 1 hour over a low–medium heat; you want to see the bubbles rising in the pot. You may need to turn halfway to ensure an even colour on the skin.

After 1 hour, check the seasoning of the braising liquid and adjust it with a generous pinch of salt, if necessary. Simmer gently over a low heat for a further 30–45 minutes until the meat is cooked through and tender, but not completely falling apart. Once finished cooking, turn off the heat and let the pork rest in the pan for 10 minutes.

Meanwhile, make the dipping sauce by combining all the sauce ingredients together in a bowl. Check for seasoning; it should be salty but balanced with acidity and sweetness. Adjust with a touch of salt, or more vinegar or sugar, if necessary.

Remove the pork from the pan and transfer to a plate. Brush the skin of the hock with the sesame oil and leave to cool a little to make it easier to slice. Discard the poaching liquid. When the meat has cooled down enough to touch, carefully carve the meat off the bone lengthways in a few segments, then cut each piece into 5mm (¼in) thick slices. Transfer the sliced hock to a large platter, arranging it to show off the beautifully glossy skin. Sprinkle with a generous pinch of sesame seeds.

Serve the sliced hock with the dipping sauce on the side. A plate of pliable seasonal leaves and *ssamjang* also make a great accompaniment, which you can find from Korean supermarkets or in my first book, *Rice Table*. Wrap each slice of meat with the leaves and a dollop of sauce to make one bite-sized parcel of *ssam*.

Soy Sauce KFC Crispy Wings

Ganjang Yangnyeom Chicken

The first time I was introduced to this version of soy sauce wings, which was ordered by my brother-in-law from one of the well-known chicken delivery chains in Korea, I was blown away by just how light and fragrant the sauce was. The craggy skin was delicately crispy with the sauce just about coating the outside to give it a moist bite; it was so addictively moreish.

While I am yet to convince myself whether I have achieved a respectful approximation of these iconic wings, I think this recipe successfully nods to them. Warming Chinese five-spice gently hums in the background of the luxurious, salty, sweet and silky sauce, which dresses the fried chicken gracefully so you can really appreciate the taste of the chicken and the crispness of its lightly crusted skin. It is wonderful served with White Cabbage Salad (page 116).

SERVES 2–4

8 chicken wings, about 800g (1lb 12oz)
vegetable oil, for frying

For the marinade
½ onion, roughly chopped
4 garlic cloves, lightly crushed
5 tbsp full-fat milk
1 tbsp golden granulated sugar
1 tsp fine sea salt
1 tsp cayenne pepper
½ tsp ground white pepper

For the soy sauce glaze
300ml (10fl oz/1¼ cups) just-boiled water
3 tbsp soft brown sugar
2 tbsp jocheong (rice syrup) or clear honey
1 tbsp Worcestershire sauce
4 tbsp soy sauce
1 tsp Chinese five-spice powder
2 garlic cloves, crushed
2 spring onions (scallions), cut in half to fit the pan
2 hot green chillies, kept whole with a small cut down the middle
2 tbsp cider vinegar

For the dry coating
75g (2½oz/scant ⅔ cup) plain (all-purpose) flour
75g (2½oz/scant ½ cup) rice flour or glutinous rice flour
½ tsp fine sea salt

Prepare the chicken wings by jointing into three parts: drumette, wingette and wingtips. You can do this by stretching out the wing and running your fingertips around the joints to identify the ridge. Using a sharp knife, cut beside the ridge to separate: one between the wingtip and wingette, and another between wingette and drumette. If you are unsure, there are many tutorial videos available online; it is a lot easier than it sounds. Or ask your butcher to do this for you. Keep aside the drumette and wingette; wingtips can be reserved for making a homemade stock for another time.

Put the onion, garlic and milk in a food processor and blitz until smooth. Pour the puréed mixture into a large mixing bowl. Whisk in the sugar, salt, cayenne pepper and white pepper to combine. Add the jointed wings to the mixing bowl. Massage well to coat the wings evenly with the marinade. Cover and leave to marinate in the fridge for a minimum of 1 hour or preferably overnight.

To make the glaze, combine the water, sugar, jocheong, Worcestershire sauce, soy sauce and Chinese five-spice powder in a small saucepan. Don't worry if the jocheong or five-spice powder don't fully incorporate initially – it will melt as it heats. Add the garlic, spring onions and chillies to the pan. Bring to the boil, then simmer for 20 minutes until the flavours of the aromatics are infused and the sauce has reduced slightly. Remove and discard the aromatics. Stir in the vinegar. Increase the heat and continue cooking on a high simmer for 8–10 minutes to thicken the sauce. It should be reduced enough to be a pourable consistency but cling to the spoon. Remove from the heat and leave to cool.

Remove the chicken from the fridge so it's not fridge cold when you cook it. Lift out the wings from the marinade; discard the marinade.

Combine the plain flour, rice flour and salt in a bowl or large reusable plastic bag. Add the wings to the dry flour mix and coat them evenly by tossing them in the bowl, or shaking the bag with the top sealed if you're using a bag. Transfer to a large tray in a single layer and rest for a few minutes, so the dry coating can settle.

Prepare a cooling rack set over a roasting tray.

Recipe continues overleaf

Fill a large, heavy-based saucepan with enough vegetable oil to submerge the wings but come no more than three-quarters of the way up the pan. Heat the oil to 150°C (300°F). Carefully lower in a few of the wings and fry for about 4 minutes until the meat is cooked through and pale golden. Transfer to the cooling rack when they're done to allow the steam to escape. Don't put too many in at once. Continue until you have cooked all the wings. This first fry is to cook the wings through, so they shouldn't take on too much colour.

Increase the oil temperature to 175°C (347°F) and fry in batches for the second time for about 2 minutes until golden brown and crispy. Make sure you don't overcrowd the pan. When the batches are ready, transfer to the cooling rack to remove any excess oil. Don't be tempted to sit the chicken on kitchen paper as it will just steam and lose its crispness.

Put the wings into a large mixing bowl and toss generously with the sauce to coat. Serve immediately with some cabbage salad and a few bottles of cold beer to create an old-school *chimaek* (fried chicken and beer) vibe.

GLUTINOUS RICE FLOUR

Glutinous flour will give a finish that is lightly crispy, while rice flour gives a more crunchy finish. It is a subtle difference, both of which are equally good.

Gochujang Pork Taco

Jeyuk Bokkeum

Quite a few years ago, when I went to Korea for my sister's wedding, the weather in Seoul was on the cusp of winter. Cool, crisp air started to turn a little nippier in the evening, and the golden-fringed ginkgo trees and sunset-shaded auburn leaves of autumn faded into brittle brown to trail our footsteps. I always think spring and autumn in Seoul are a particularly good time to stroll around exploring the city and discovering its less-trodden side streets, often enticed by the delicious-smelling air that tickles the appetite.

This dish is inspired by a spicy *gochujang*-marinated pork I ate on one of those evenings. My completely unplanned leisurely stroll ended up in a small charcoal grill joint under a thick tarpaulin-roofed balcony. The glowing embers warmed our cheeks to take the edge off the chill in the air and the sweet-scented meat sizzled and caramelized, thick smoke rising up to lace the flesh. I came home wanting to recreate the flavours and the cosiness of that evening.

The melt-in-your-mouth tender pork, wrapped with a molasses-like depth of sweet and smoky flavour, eats well with rice but is even better served with small tortilla breads as tacos. It's the kind of dish I love to cook to feast with friends and family. *Pictured overleaf.*

SERVES 4 GENEROUSLY

2 tbsp vegetable oil
2 onions, thinly sliced
sea salt flakes, to taste
800g (1lb 12oz) pork shoulder joint without rind but with a little layer of fat on top
2 dried bay leaves

For the sauce
½ apple, roughly chopped
4 garlic cloves, crushed
2 tsp chopped root ginger
2 tbsp mirin
1 heaped tbsp dark soft brown sugar
3 tbsp *gochugaru* (Korean red pepper flakes)
3 tbsp *gochujang* (Korean fermented chilli paste)
2 tbsp soy sauce
2 tbsp blackstrap molasses
250ml (9fl oz/2 cups) just-boiled water

For the pickled onion
1 red onion, thinly sliced
60ml (2fl oz/¼ cup) water
1 tbsp golden granulated sugar
¼ tsp sea salt flakes
1 dried red chilli
1 strip of lemon peel
2 tbsp cider vinegar

To finish
warm tortilla breads, lime wedges and sour cream

Preheat the oven to 150°C fan (160°C/300°F/gas 2).

To make the sauce, place the apple, garlic, ginger and mirin in a food processor and blend to a smooth purée. Transfer to a mixing bowl and add the rest of the sauce ingredients, including the water. Combine well and set aside.

Heat the vegetable oil in a large, lidded casserole dish over a low heat and sauté the onions with a pinch of salt for 15 minutes until the onions are softened and lightly caramelized. Add the pork and bay leaves, and pour the sauce over and around the pork. Increase the heat to bring to a simmer.

Scrunch up a large sheet of parchment paper and run it under cold water. Squeeze out the excess water and make a drop lid by laying the parchment paper right on top of the food to cover. Place the casserole lid on top and transfer to the oven. Leave to cook for 3 hours, stirring halfway through.

Meanwhile, to make the pickled onion, put the red onion in a heatproof bowl or container. Combine the water, sugar, salt and dried chilli in a small saucepan and gently heat to dissolve the sugar. Add the lemon peel and stir in the vinegar. Pour the warm liquid over the onion. Set aside to cool, then cover and refrigerate until needed.

After 3 hours, the pork should be meltingly tender. Discard the bay leaves and carefully lift out the meat onto a tray or chopping board. Skim off some of the excess fat from the sauce, if there's too much.

Pull the meat apart with a couple of forks, then stir it back into the sauce. Transfer the pulled meat onto a sharing platter and serve warm with a side of pickled onion, plus soft tortilla breads, lime wedges for squeezing over, and some sour cream to offset the heat.

Gochujang Rose Chicken

Rose Chicken

Rose sauce – also known as parma rosa sauce or pink sauce – is more commonly associated with Italian pasta. But this tangy, tomato-based sauce enriched with a blend of cream and cheese seems to have well and truly embedded itself in the modern Korean food scene in recent years. Countless variations of the original sauce have been created by using more locally available ingredients, such as *gochujang* to replace tomato.

While rose *tteokbokki* or *gochujang* rose pasta dishes are what possibly pushed the fame of this Korean adaptation of creamy salmon pink-hued sauce right up to the top, I actually rather like it over a pan-fried chicken. It makes a great one-pan meal that eats well with a side of oven fries and a simple green salad.

SERVES 2–4

about 650g (1lb 7oz) boneless, skin-on chicken thighs
sea salt flakes
1 tbsp extra virgin olive oil
4 garlic cloves, thinly sliced
30g (1oz) onion or shallot, finely minced
2 tbsp *gochujang* (Korean fermented chilli paste)
1 tsp *gochugaru* (Korean red pepper flakes)
180ml (6fl oz/¾ cup) dry white wine
150ml (5fl oz/scant ⅔ cup) double (heavy) cream
1 tbsp Worcestershire sauce
½ tsp freshly cracked black pepper
30g (1oz) parmesan, grated
2 tsp snipped chives

Pat the chicken dry with kitchen paper and season with a generous pinch of salt. If you have time, leave the seasoned chicken uncovered in the fridge overnight; it will help to dry the skin, which will give you a crispier finish. If you're pushed for time, just move on to the next step.

Heat the olive oil in a heavy-based sauté pan over a low–medium heat. Add the garlic and fry for 2 minutes until lightly golden and crispy, not dark brown as it will become unpleasantly bitter. You may need to tilt the pan a little to pool the oil to help the garlic to fry. Once done, transfer to a plate lined with kitchen paper. Set aside until needed.

Lower the heat a touch. Put the chicken into the same pan skin-side down. Place another frying pan or saucepan on top to press the chicken. Cook the meat for about 12 minutes until the skin is nicely seared and crisp. The chicken should be about 60 per cent cooked. Carefully turn the chicken over to the meat side and continue cooking (without the pan pressing) until the chicken is cooked through (about 4 minutes). Once done, transfer to a plate, leave to rest and keep warm while you get on with the sauce.

Reduce the heat immediately. Add the onion to the pan with a little pinch of salt and sauté for about a minute to soften. Stir in the *gochujang* and *gochugaru*, and cook for 1 minute to bring out the flavour. Add the white wine and stir to combine. Increase the heat and let it bubble for about 3 minutes until the wine has reduced by half. Stir in the cream, Worcestershire sauce, black pepper and parmesan, and simmer steadily to reduce and thicken to a pourable sauce consistency. Check for seasoning and adjust it with a pinch of salt. Stir in most of the chopped chives, reserving some for the garnish.

Pour the sauce onto individual plates or a serving platter. Slice the chicken into 2cm (¾in) thick pieces and arrange it on top of the sauce. Scatter with the reserved fried garlic and chives. Enjoy while warm.

Chuncheon-Style Spicy Stir-Fried Chicken

Chuncheon Dakgalbi

I often think the star of this dish is actually the cabbage, and the rice that is fried in the sauce towards the end, bringing a satisfying finish to the meal. The gentle vegetal flavour of cabbage works brilliantly, comfortably carrying the bold, spicy seasoning laced with curry powder, which is unique to the Chuncheon style of *dakgalbi*. The perfectly scorched, starchy grains are bound by the remnants of salty umami sweetness – it is hard not to dig straight in with the spoon to scrape off the crispy bits before anyone else gets there. It's an easy, sociable one-pan dish, typically cooked at the table.

SERVES 4

600g (1lb 5oz) boneless
   chicken thighs
   (or leg meat)
250g (9oz) white cabbage
1 sweet potato
200g (7oz) cylinder-shaped
   rice cakes (fresh or frozen)
4 spring onions (scallions)
15 perilla leaves
1 mild green chilli
2 tbsp vegetable oil
sea salt flakes, to taste

For the marinade

1 onion, roughly chopped
½ apple (a sweet variety
   such as fuji or gala),
   roughly chopped
5 garlic cloves, crushed
2 tsp grated root ginger
2 tbsp mirin
4 tbsp soy sauce
2 tbsp *gochugaru* (Korean
   red pepper flakes)
2 tbsp light soft brown sugar
1 tbsp *gochujang* (Korean
   fermented chilli paste)
2 tsp toasted sesame oil
1 tsp mild curry powder
½ tsp freshly cracked
   black pepper

Remove the skin from the chicken, if preferred, and slice into bite-sized chunks, about 3cm (1¼in) square. Transfer to a large mixing bowl.

Purée the onion, apple, garlic, ginger and mirin in a food processor until smooth, then pour over the chicken. Add the rest of the ingredients for the marinade to the bowl and massage well – ideally by hand – to evenly coat the meat. Cover and refrigerate while you get on with the rest of the prep, or leave to marinate overnight, if you wish.

Meanwhile, prepare the vegetables: roughly chop or tear the cabbage into large bite-sized pieces. Peel the sweet potato, if you prefer, then slice into rounds about 5mm (¼in) thick. Soak the rice cakes in cold water, if using frozen, then drain and set aside. Slice the spring onions into 5cm (2in) long batons. Trim the top of the perilla leaves, then cut them into quarters. Thinly slice the chilli.

Remove the marinated chicken from the fridge.

Heat the vegetable oil in a heavy-based frying pan (skillet) over a medium heat and add the chicken, including the marinade, evenly across the pan. Notice the sizzling sound. Layer on top the cabbage, sweet potato and rice cakes. Cook without disturbing for 2 minutes to lightly colour the bottom side of the chicken, then flip and toss everything together. The pan may appear quite dry to start with but don't worry; as the vegetables start to cook, they will release enough water to bring everything together. Stir continuously and energetically to prevent the mixture from burning or browning too quickly. Continue to cook in this way for 8–10 minutes until the chicken has almost cooked through and the cabbage pieces have collapsed. Stir in the spring onions and perilla leaves and continue stir-frying for about 5 minutes until the chicken and rice cakes are cooked through. Scatter with the sliced green chilli before removing from the heat. Check for seasoning and adjust it with a pinch of salt if needed. Serve immediately in a family style for everyone to help themselves.

PERILLA LEAVES

Perilla leaves can be found in Korean supermarkets. If you can't get hold of them, just leave them out, or if you have perilla oil handy, a few drops at the end of cooking can add a similar aroma to the dish.

FRIED RICE

A common practice is often to fry some rice in the sauce towards the end of the dish when you have eaten almost all the meat but there is still enough sauce left to fill a rice bowl. To enjoy this wonderful part of Korean food culture, add one serving of cooked rice to the pan, along with some sesame oil, roughly chopped soft salad leaves and a big fistful of *gim jaban* (crumbled toasted seasoned seaweed). Stir-fry over a medium heat and flatten to spread thinly in the middle of the pan. Let it cook for a couple of minutes to gently scorch the bottom, then serve straight away.

Ketchup Fried Frankfurters

Sausage Yachae Bokkeum

I used to think it was my lucky day when my school lunch box was packed with these little bite-sized sausages smothered in a sweet, vinegary ketchup sauce. Little did I know back then, it was also favoured by many as a beer snack. Perfectly hasselbacked sausages open up to catch the tangy, salty-sweet sauce in the pockets; the sweet acidity complements the smoky flavours with the cooked onions and peppers leaving a touch of freshness to balance. It's still one of the most loved cheap and cheerful old-school beer snacks.

SERVES 4

350g (12oz) frankfurters
2 tbsp tomato
    ketchup (catsup)
1 tbsp golden granulated
    sugar
1 tbsp soy sauce
1 tbsp Worcestershire sauce
1 tsp oyster sauce
1 tbsp vegetable oil
4 garlic cloves, thinly sliced
½ red onion, sliced
150g (5oz) green (bell)
    peppers, sliced
1 red chilli, sliced
½ tsp freshly cracked
    black pepper
1 tsp toasted white
    sesame seeds

Slice the frankfurters in half, then in half again so you have bite-sized pieces about 4cm (1½in) long. Make parallel cuts on top of each piece – as you would with hasselback potatoes – about one-third of the way down and 1–2mm apart. You should be able to cut a few pieces together at the same time.

Combine the ketchup, sugar, soy sauce, Worcestershire sauce and oyster sauce in a small bowl.

Heat the vegetable oil in a wok or frying pan (skillet) over a medium heat. Add the garlic and sauté briefly until fragrant and softened. Add the frankfurters, onion, peppers and chilli and stir-fry for about 3 minutes until the sausages have cooked through and the onions and peppers have cooked enough but still have a little bite to them.

Add the ketchup seasoning and black pepper and continue to cook for 2 minutes, stirring energetically to coat everything evenly. As the sugar starts to cook, you should notice the sweet aromas of caramelization. When the sauce has reduced to coat everything in a glossy glaze, remove from the heat and stir in the sesame seeds. Serve warm as a beer snack or with some plain steamed rice.

Soul Session – Sharing Pots

Koreans are a nation known to love bubbling hot broths. Enter the world of popular soups and stews that are good enough to be a meal on their own.

Army Stew

Budae Jjigae

When you think about what constitutes *budae jjigae* (more commonly known as army stew in the West), at face value it has every element of a hearty and comforting sausage stew. The combination of salty ham with the depth of Korean spicing creates a dish that is layered with some big bold flavours. But weaving through the spoonful of unctuously rich and spicy stew is the taste of a difficult history. The scarcity of food supplies after the Korean War meant many people had to be reliant on what little was around and make even that stretch a long way. Smuggled goods from locally based US army surplus supplies and scraps became the main food source for many. People adopted previously alien ingredients, such as canned meats and beans, and had to become creative with them to make their food palatable.

Heavily engulfed in a harrowing history, certain generations choke at the mention of this dish. But for others, it is a soulful reminder of important events in the past and is enjoyed with deep appreciation. Army stew, for me, feels like a taste of strength; it demonstrates the inherently resourceful and adaptive nature of Korean cuisine. And I think the dish should be celebrated, not only for its robust flavours but also for its origin, which represents the heart of the resilient and hopeful nation. *Pictured overleaf.*

SERVES 4

3 spring onions (scallions)
150g (5oz) sliced rice cakes (frozen or fresh)
1 onion, thinly sliced
150g (5oz) cabbage kimchi, roughly chopped
200g (7oz) canned Spam, sliced into 5mm (¼in) thick slabs
4 frankfurters, sliced 1cm (½in) thick at an angle
100g (3½oz) baked beans
200g (7oz) tofu, sliced 1cm (½in) thick
800ml (28fl oz/3½ cups) just-boiled water
sea salt flakes, to taste
1 pack of Korean instant noodles (I like Shin or Ansungtangmyun)
1 mild green chilli, sliced

For the sauce
4 garlic cloves, minced
1½ tbsp *gochugaru* (Korean red pepper flakes)
1½ tbsp light or soup soy sauce
1 tbsp *gochujang* (Korean fermented chilli paste)
1 tbsp *yondu* (seasoning sauce)
1 tbsp fish sauce
½ tsp golden granulated sugar
½ tsp freshly cracked black pepper

Slice the spring onions into 5cm (2in) long batons; halve the white parts lengthways if too thick and slice the green parts at an angle. Transfer the green parts to a bowl with cold water and leave to soak while you get on with the rest of the dish. Soak the rice cakes in cold water for 10 minutes, if using frozen.

Scatter the sliced onion over the bottom of a large, shallow, rimmed, flameproof casserole dish with a lid and arrange the kimchi, Spam, frankfurters, baked beans, tofu and white parts of the spring onions attractively on top, leaving some space to accommodate the rice cakes and noodles later.

Put all the ingredients for the sauce in a mixing bowl and stir together well, then gently pour this over the neatly arranged ingredients in the casserole dish along with the just-boiled water. Place the dish over a medium heat with the lid on. Bring to the boil, then simmer for 15 minutes with the lid on ajar.

Meanwhile, drain the spring onion greens and rice cakes. Set aside.

After 15 minutes, the stew should have reduced and thickened slightly with all the flavours mingling together. Check for seasoning and adjust it with a pinch of salt or sugar, if necessary. Make a space in the pan where appropriate and add the noodles (discarding the packet of sauce that comes with them) and rice cakes. Top with the green chilli and the spring onion greens. Continue simmering for 4–5 minutes until the noodles and rice cakes are cooked through. Remove from the heat and serve immediately straight from the pan while bubbling hot.

Fishcake Soup

Eomuktang

For me, winter in Korea is filled with deliciously comforting smells. There are long queues for vendors selling fried pancakes filled with molten hot sugar that always burns the roof of my mouth; slowly roasting chestnuts in open fires keep me warm just looking at them. Every street corner is chock full of hazy steam, and the street-food carts always feel like an inviting place to gather to warm up, to allow ourselves a moment of simple joy.

A ladleful of braised fishcake broth in a paper cup is what I remember most about Korean winters. Held tightly with icy-cold hands, the warmth of the broth soon radiates as you eagerly blow into the cup. With white steam caressing cold cheeks, soothing flavours of warm ocean-like saltiness hug the mouth with their rich and savoury hum. You can taste the faint sweetness of radish coming in and out like gentle waves. Before you know it, your appetite is suitably teased and stiff fingers are softened enough to manoeuvre the skewers of tenderly braised fishcakes into the vinegary dipping sauce to season each bite perfectly. This is cheap and cheerful comfort and I cannot imagine a winter without it.

The recipe here is a single serving, mainly because it is what I make myself for lunch when cold weather calls for something warming and comforting in a hurry. But you can easily multiply the recipe to feed a crowd. Korean fishcakes are usually found in freezer sections in Korean or other Asian supermarkets. I use the flat rectangular sheets but other shapes work fine too.

SERVES 1

You will need 2 short
  wooden skewers

300ml (10fl oz/1¼ cups)
  warm water
60g (2oz) daikon radish,
  cut into 1cm (½in)
  thick batons
20g (¾oz) onion,
  thinly sliced
one 5×7.5cm (2×3in) sheet
  of *dasima* (dried kelp)
1 tbsp fish sauce
1 tbsp mirin
2 sheets of frozen fishcakes
¼ tsp ground white pepper
½ spring onion (scallion),
  thinly sliced

For the dipping sauce
1 tbsp soy sauce
1 tbsp cider vinegar
1 tsp golden granulated
  sugar
1 tbsp water
½ tsp wasabi paste
  (optional)

Put the water, daikon radish, onion, *dasima*, fish sauce and mirin into a heavy-based saucepan with a lid. Bring just to the boil, cover with a lid, then reduce the heat to simmer gently for 15 minutes.

Meanwhile, plunge the frozen fishcake sheets in hot water for 1 minute. Drain and fold in half lengthways. Hold one of the folded fishcake sheets in your less dominant hand and thread onto the first skewer, pleating about every 2.5cm (1in) as you go along. Repeat with the second skewer.

Make the dipping sauce by combining all the sauce ingredients in a small bowl. Set aside.

After 15 minutes, the vegetables should have softened and their flavours been extracted. Scoop out the *dasima* and discard. Check for seasoning and adjust it with a touch more fish sauce, or a pinch of salt, if you like. Add the fishcake skewers, ensuring the fishcakes are mostly submerged in the broth. Simmer gently for a further 5 minutes until the fishcakes are cooked. Stir in the white pepper and remove from the heat. Transfer to your favourite soup bowl. Scatter with the spring onion and eat while steaming hot, dunking the fishcake skewers into the dipping sauce in between spoonfuls of broth. Feel the warmth that radiates from the streets of Seoul on a blisteringly cold winter's day.

Soju Steamed Mussels + Broth

Honghaptang

Steamed mussels of any kind are just a classic – a fail-safe, simple and delicious dish.

In Korea, the dish became the cornerstone of the pocha menu, as a bag of mussels used to cost next to nothing – so little, in fact, that a ladleful of mussels in broth would be offered to the table free of charge as a gesture of good and generous hospitality.

A glistening pile of plump mussels bathing in a pool of aromatic milky broth is still a common sight at many pocha joints, especially in colder months as mussels in season are inexpensive and bountiful. While modern-day stalls may find it challenging to stretch quite as far as a free bowl of mussels (with the rise of running costs), the warming broth is always offered plentifully, for diners to joyfully slurp away, in the same spirit of generosity.

Serve with Lazy Oven Chips + Magic Savoury Salt (page 164) to make it an easy weeknight supper.

SERVES 2–4

½ onion, peeled and
  left whole
2 spring onions (scallions),
  white parts cut into
  batons, green parts thinly
  sliced for garnish
4 garlic cloves,
  lightly crushed
800ml (28fl oz/3½ cups)
  just-boiled water
1 kg (2lb 4oz) mussels,
  scrubbed and
  beards removed
125ml (4fl oz/½ cup) soju
1 red chilli, thinly sliced
1 tsp sea salt flakes
¼ tsp ground white pepper

Put the onion, the white parts of the spring onions and the garlic into a lidded, heavy-based saucepan with the water. Put the lid on and bring to the boil, then simmer the stock for 20 minutes with the lid on ajar over a low heat until the vegetables are softened and their flavours extracted. Scoop out and discard the aromatics.

Discard any mussels that remain open and put the rest into the saucepan with the stock and soju. Put the lid back on and crank up the heat to bring just to the boil, then simmer gently for about 5 minutes until the shells have opened. Discard any that remain closed.

Add the red chilli and stir in the salt and white pepper. Check for seasoning and adjust it with a pinch more salt, if necessary, before removing from the heat. Scatter with the reserved green parts of the spring onions. Serve immediately while steaming hot and slurp away the delicious broth.

Gochujang Stew

Gochujang Jjigae

Also known as *jjageuli* or camping stew – as campers used to make it with whatever they had on hand – *gochujang* stew is often praised for its versatility to accommodate any odds and ends of vegetables, meat or fish. It is boldly seasoned and the starch from the potatoes naturally thickens the broth with a touch of creaminess. Its unctuously smoky heat clings to the mouth like a warm blanket and finishes with the trails of rounded sweetness that linger on, thanks to the soft alliums and cabbage.

Embrace its adaptive nature and swap the vegetables and proteins with whatever is in season; mussels, prawns, clams or even canned tuna can be thrown into the pool of crimson red deliciousness. Minced (ground) meat can also replace the strips of meat. I like the neutral taste of white cabbage in winter for its gentle, vegetal sweetness that carries the strong flavours so well, but in summer sweet courgettes (zucchini), stewed until tender in *gochujang*, brightens up the dish, making it a cosy, rainy-day food.

SERVES 4

1 tbsp vegetable oil
1 tbsp toasted sesame oil
250g (9oz) rib-eye steak
    or bavette, sliced into
    thin strips
½ onion, sliced
4 garlic cloves, minced
3 tbsp *gochujang* (Korean
    fermented chilli paste)
1 tbsp *gochugaru* (Korean
    red pepper flakes)
1 tbsp light or soup soy sauce
1 tbsp fish sauce
250g (9oz) floury potatoes,
    cut into large chunks
250g (9oz) white cabbage
    or courgettes (zucchini),
    cut into chunks
200g (7oz) tomatoes,
    skinned and quartered
700ml (24fl oz/scant 3 cups)
    just-boiled water
200g (7oz) tofu, cut into
    bite-sized cubes
sea salt flakes, to taste
80g (3oz) watercress,
    roughly chopped
2 spring onions (scallions),
    sliced diagonally
1 mild or hot green
    chilli, sliced

Heat the vegetable and sesame oils in a large, lidded, heavy-based saucepan. Add the beef and onion and sauté over a medium heat for about 4 minutes until the meat is browned a little and the onions are softened. Lower the heat a touch and add the garlic and *gochujang*. Continue cooking for about 5 minutes, stirring occasionally to stop it from burning. You should notice the rich crimson-red oil separating in the pan and everything smelling deliciously fragrant.

Stir in the *gochugaru*, soy sauce and fish sauce. Add the potatoes, cabbage, tomatoes and water and bring just to the boil, then simmer gently for 15 minutes with the lid on ajar.

Add the tofu and cook for a further 10 minutes until everything is tender and the tofu has absorbed the flavour.

Check for seasoning and adjust with a pinch of salt. Reserve some of the watercress and spring onions for the garnish and add the rest to the pan with the chilli. Cover with the lid and simmer gently for 3–5 minutes to soften.

Divide the stew into four deep bowls. Top with the reserved watercress and spring onions. Serve immediately while steaming hot with plain steamed rice.

Seoul-Style Bulgogi

Seoulsik Bulgogi

Seoul-style *bulgogi* – also commonly known as *yetnal* (old-school) *bulgogi* – is presented noticeably differently from the other regional varieties. Famous for its brothy hotpot style, the meat is usually cooked on a dome-shaped pan with holes that enable the subtle fragrance of smoke to lace the dish, while the rimmed surrounds of the pan hold the base stock, effectively collecting the meat juices and drippings to further season during cooking. It boasts a broth that is balanced with pronounced sweet and salty umami notes and calls for pearly white grains of steamed rice to smoosh everything together. it's a delicious brown mess that gives comfort with every mouthful.

The best quality of meat for *bulgogi* has good marbling with thin layers of fat. Beef is cut wafer thin, so thin you can easily tear the meat with a gentle touch of the fingers. Long marination isn't necessary here, with some actually preferring to only dress the meat right before cooking.

You can find pre-sliced beef for *bulgogi* in the freezer section of Korean grocers. I have found that thinly sliced beef labelled as 'for *shabu shabu*' or '*sukiyaki*' also make a good substitute. If you would like to slice the meat at home, wrap the piece tightly with clingfilm (plastic wrap) and freeze for an hour or so until partially frozen. The meat should be firm but not rock solid, just enough to make it easier to run the knife through. Unwrap the clingfilm and – carefully and patiently – slice the meat against the grain as thinly as possible – about 1–1.5mm thick – with a sharp knife or mandoline.

SERVES 4

100g (3½oz) *dangmyeon* (Korean sweet potato vermicelli noodles), optional
500g (1lb 2oz) *bulgogi* beef or thick-cut ribeye, chuck or sirloin, sliced wafer thin
1 onion, thinly sliced
200g (7oz) sliced mixed mushrooms such as oyster, shiitake, enoki or shimeji
3 spring onions (scallions), sliced 1cm (½in) thick diagonally
sea salt flakes, to taste

For the base stock
one 2.5cm (1in) square piece of *dasima* (dried kelp)
1 tbsp *yondu* (seasoning sauce)
½ tsp Marmite (yeast extract)
200ml (7fl oz/scant 1 cup) warm water

For the marinade
½ onion, roughly chopped
½ Asian pear, peeled, cored and roughly chopped (if unavailable, use other sweet varieties or apple)
2 garlic cloves, lightly crushed
2 tsp sliced root ginger
1 tbsp soft brown sugar
3 tbsp sake
3 tbsp soy sauce
2 tbsp mirin
1 tbsp *jocheong* (Korean rice syrup) or neutral-tasting honey
1 tbsp toasted sesame oil
½ tsp freshly cracked black pepper

Soak the *dangmyeon* in cold water for 20 minutes then drain, if using.

Prepare the base stock by placing *dasima*, *yondu*, Marmite and water in a small, lidded saucepan. Stir to combine and let it gently steep on a low simmer for 15 minutes with the lid on while you get on with the rest.

To make the marinade, place the onion, pear, garlic, ginger, sugar and sake into a food processor. Blend until smooth, then stir in the soy sauce, mirin, *jocheong*, sesame oil and black pepper. Combine well.

Pat the beef dry with kitchen paper to remove any sitting blood. Transfer to a large mixing bowl and gently shake the meat to separate. Pour the marinade over the beef and massage together by hand to evenly coat the meat.

To assemble the dish, layer a flameproof shallow casserole dish with the sliced onions at the bottom, then spread the marinated beef at the centre on top of the onions, leaving some space around the edges. Fill the edges with the mushrooms, *dangmyeon*, if using, and spring onions, reserving some of the green parts for the garnish.

By now, the base stock should be ready. Discard the *dasima* and carefully pour the stock into the side of the casserole pan. Bring the mixture to just boiling, then simmer steadily over a medium heat for 8–10 minutes until the noodles are cooked and the beef meltingly tender. Check for seasoning and adjust it with a pinch of salt, if necessary. Remove from the heat. Scatter with the reserved spring onions and serve immediately, ideally with a bowl of steamed rice.

Pork Bone + Potato Stew

Gamjatang

The name *gamjatang* often causes confusion as its more common translation would be a potato stew – *gamja* being a Korean word for potato – whereas in this recipe, it's the bones that are the star of the dish. The story goes that the name actually originates from the fact that the spinal cord in the pig's backbone is also called *gamja*.

More traditionally, the dish calls for pork backbone, which includes the meatier neck bones. Collagen-rich bones and connective tissues yield a naturally thickened, milky broth and deeply flavoursome stew. You can ask for the neck bones from a good butcher or find them in the freezer section of Korean supermarkets, often labelled as 'pork bones for *gamjatang*', which have a decent bit of meat left on them to eat. In case you can't find either, I have found loin ribs, also known as baby back ribs, make a reasonable substitution.

SERVES 4–6

250g (9oz) pak choi (bok choy)
1–1.3kg (2lb 4oz–2lb 8oz) pork bones (neck, back or loin ribs – see intro)
1.8 litres (60fl oz/ 7½ cups) water
sea salt flakes, to taste

For the seasoning paste
1 onion, roughly chopped
30g (1oz) garlic, crushed
10g (¼oz) root ginger, roughly sliced
2 mild green chillies (serrano or jalapeños), sliced
1 mild red chilli, sliced
3 tbsp *gochugaru* (Korean red pepper flakes)
2 tbsp *doenjang* (Korean fermented bean paste)
2 tbsp light or soup soy sauce
2 tbsp *yondu*
2 tbsp mirin
1 tsp golden granulated sugar
½ tsp shrimp paste
½ tsp ground white pepper

For the vegetables
500g (1lb 2oz) waxy or semi-waxy potatoes, such as Yukon gold, peeled
4 spring onions (scallions)
15 perilla leaves (or 50g/ 2oz watercress)

To finish
2 tbsp ground sesame seeds
a few drops of perilla oil

Trim off the root end of the pak choi and pull apart the leaves. Bring a large pan of water to the boil; we will use the same pan for blanching the pork bones so make sure the pan is large enough to accommodate all the bones. Also have a bowl of cold water ready close by, so you can plunge the blanched pak choi immediately into the cold water. When the water is rapidly boiling, carefully drop in the pak choi and blanch for 1 minute until a little floppy. Lift out the wilted greens and transfer to the bowl of cold water to stop the cooking, then drain. Gently squeeze the water out of the pak choi by hand, without squashing the leaves too much. Separate the leaves and tear the larger leaves lengthways. Set aside.

In the same pan, blanch the bones uncovered, for 5–10 minutes, depending on the size and types of bones you're using. You will notice a foamy brown scum appears on the surface. Carefully drain the water out and rinse the bones under cold water, ensuring the bones are clean and free of all scum. Drain. Put the drained bones into a heavy-based lidded casserole dish and fill with the measured cold water. Bring to a boil, then simmer steadily for 1 hour with the lid on ajar.

Meanwhile, prepare the seasoning paste by blending the onion, garlic, ginger and both chillies in a food processor until smooth. Pour the puréed mixture into a large mixing bowl and combine with the rest of the ingredients for the seasoning paste. Add the blanched pak choi to the bowl and toss to coat. Set aside.

Prepare the vegetables. Halve the small potatoes and quarter the large ones so they are cut fairly chunky. Slice 3 spring onions diagonally about 1cm (½in) thick and thinly slice the remaining spring onion to use as garnish later. Roughly chop 12 perilla leaves and slice the remaining 3 leaves into fine strips to use as garnish. (If using watercress, roughly chop and reserve a small amount for the garnish.)

After 1 hour, check to see if the bones are cooked just enough; the meat should be coming away from the bones and the broth should appear lightly milky in colour. Add the seasoned pak choi and the potatoes. Let it come up to just below boiling, then continue simmering for 25 minutes until the potatoes are tender.

Check for seasoning and adjust with a pinch of salt, if necessary. Stir in the thicker-sliced spring onions and the roughly chopped perilla leaves (or watercress), and simmer for 5 minutes to soften. Remove from the heat and decide if you'll serve family style or divide the stew among individual bowls. Top with the reserved sliced spring onion and perilla leaves. Scatter with the ground sesame seeds and a few drops of perilla oil just before serving.

Spicy Cod Stew

Daegu Maeuntang

My first memories of *maeuntang* go back to early morning visits to Noryangin fish market with my family at weekends, where we used to feast on a bubbling hot dish of crimson red fish stew after a platter full of fresh-off-the-boat raw fish called *hoe*. The stew was made using the remainder of our fish bought straight from the sellers in the market, usually with head and bones, and sometimes also with roe and/or innards. The dish was a good example of the 'waste-nothing' culture that is engrained in Korean cuisine: inherently frugal and resourceful nose-to-tail cooking.

Seasoned boldly with *gochugaru* and *gochujang*, the taste of *maeuntang* lives up to its name – which translates as spicy stew – with a glowing heat that catches at the back of the throat. The flavours are addictive, with fragrant allium and fish-based seasoning building to salivating umami. And this is especially true if you use the fish head; there is an old proverb in Korea that goes something like 'the flavour of fish is in the head and meat in the tail'.

I think cod is a good place to start; its mild and sweet flesh pairs well with spicy, salty seasoning. I am also hoping the familiar taste of cod will help the dish feel less alien, if this is new to you. But by all means, use whatever firm white fish are available to you.

SERVES 4

500g (1lb 2oz) skinless cod, sliced 2.5cm (1in) thick
1 tsp fine sea salt
½ tbsp perilla oil
½ tbsp vegetable oil
½ onion, sliced
2 spring onions (scallions), sliced; green parts reserved for garnish
sea salt flakes
200g (7oz) daikon radish, diced into 1cm (½in) cubes
two 5×7.5cm (2×3in) sheets of *dasima* (dried kelp)
1 litre (34fl oz/4 cups) just-boiled water
200g (7oz) courgettes (zucchini), diced into 1cm (½in) cubes
80g (3oz) watercress, roughly chopped
1 mild red chilli, sliced

For the seasoning paste
2 tbsp *gochugaru* (Korean red pepper flakes)
2 tbsp mirin
1 tbsp light or soup soy sauce
1 tbsp fish sauce
1 tbsp *gochujang* (Korean fermented chilli paste)
½ tsp shrimp paste
¼ tsp ground white pepper
4 garlic cloves, minced
1 tsp grated root ginger

Pat the fish dry with kitchen paper and lay it on a flat tray in one single layer. Sprinkle evenly with the fine salt; this will help the flesh of the fish to firm up so it doesn't completely fall apart when added to the stew. Refrigerate uncovered while you get on with the rest of the prep.

Heat both the perilla and vegetable oils in a heavy-based saucepan with a lid and sauté the onions and the white parts of the spring onions with a good pinch of salt over a low heat for 5 minutes until softened. Add the radish and give it a brief stir to coat. Add the *dasima* and water. Bring to the boil, then simmer gently over a low heat for 20 minutes with the lid on ajar.

Meanwhile, prepare the seasoning paste by combining all the paste ingredients in a small mixing bowl. Set aside.

After 20 minutes, you should notice the wonderfully fragrant smell of the stock. Scoop out and discard the *dasima*. Add the seasoning paste and give it a good stir to combine well. Add the courgettes, then increase the heat to medium and simmer steadily for 5 minutes, with the lid on ajar, until the vegetables are tender. Stir in the cod and continue simmering for a further 5 minutes until the fish is cooked through and beautifully flaking away. Check for seasoning and adjust it with a pinch more salt, if necessary. Stir in the watercress and top with the chilli and reserved green parts of the spring onions. Remove from the heat and leave to stand for 5 minutes with the lid on to gently infuse the flavours of watercress, chilli and spring onions in a residual heat, before serving.

Carby Slurps

Late-night noodles are often enjoyed to sober up after an evening of drinking, filling the belly with starchy comfort.

Perilla Oil Noodles

Deulgireum Bibim Guksu

My maternal grandmother used to fill her fields with rows and rows of perilla plants that grew like a small forest to the eyes of a child. Extended family gathered every harvesting season to pick and sort; the fruitful yield of freshly pressed oil was never in short supply. I don't think I truly appreciated the incredible taste of perilla oil until I was much older, despite having grown up with it. Back then, the oil was oil and I did not necessarily pay any particular attention to why my mother favoured it over more common sesame oil in some dishes such as *bibim guksu*, nor could I differentiate the flavours.

The anise-laced, cumin-like perfume of earthy perilla oil here is the queen that binds these cold, beautifully silky noodles, made especially rich and luxurious with golden, raw egg yolk. It is deceptively simple, yet extremely satisfying. The piquant acidity of kimchi pairs really nicely.

SERVES 2

2 servings of thin wheat
  noodles or soba noodles
sea salt flakes, to taste

For the dressing
1 tbsp cider vinegar
1 tbsp toasted white sesame
  seeds, lightly crushed,
  plus extra for garnish
2 tbsp golden granulated
  sugar
3 tbsp soy sauce
4 tbsp perilla oil
2 garlic cloves, grated
2 spring onions (scallions),
  thinly sliced
2 hot green chillies,
  thinly sliced
½ tsp freshly cracked
  black pepper

For the garnish
80g (3oz) cucumber,
  julienned thinly
a small handful
  of salad cress
2 egg yolks (optional)
2 tbsp *gim jaban*
  (crumbled toasted
  seasoned seaweed)

Combine all the dressing ingredients in a large mixing bowl big enough to accommodate the noodles, so you can toss them directly in the bowl. Give it a good stir to dissolve the sugar, then set aside.

Cook the noodles according to the packet instructions. Rinse well under cold running water to remove the starch, then drain thoroughly. Transfer the drained noodles to the mixing bowl with the dressing and toss the noodles, preferably by hand, to distribute the sauce evenly. Check the seasoning and adjust with a pinch of salt, if necessary. When done, divide between two bowls and top with the cucumber, salad cress, egg yolks, if using, and *gim jaban*. Sprinkle with the extra sesame seeds to finish.

Sweet Potato Noodles + Vegetables

Japchae

When I was growing up, this glorious mess of jumbled noodles and rainbow vegetables used to be the crowning jewel of occasions that required the go-all-out kind of feasting in our household, be it a family gathering, house-warming party or holidays. Renowned for its fiddly process, traditionally, more elaborate varieties of vegetables are prepared and seasoned separately before being tossed together with noodles. Nowadays, many opt to cook the dish in a much simplified way by stir-frying everything together to enjoy as an easy meal.

But when I think of *japchae*, the real joy is in the process, which brings back early memories of making the dish with my mother. The sensation that I felt through my fingertips is still so vivid, palms warm and soft from gently tossing the noodles. The irresistible aromas of roasted sesame oil glossed my lips as I treated myself to the first bite and the vegetables waltzed across my mouth, caressed softly in the arms of springy noodles that ate like savoury jelly. I like to keep the combination of vegetables simple, using what I have on hand.

SERVES 2–4

200g (7oz) *dangmyeon* (Korean sweet potato vermicelli noodles)
vegetable oil, for cooking
½ onion, thinly sliced
sea salt flakes, to taste
80g (3oz) carrot, julienned
1 long red chilli, halved and julienned
2 mild green chillies, halved and julienned
3 garlic cloves, minced
1 tsp golden granulated sugar
3 tbsp soy sauce
2 tbsp toasted sesame oil
2 tsp toasted white sesame seeds

For the mushrooms
25g (1oz) dried shiitake mushrooms
2 garlic cloves, finely minced
1½ tbsp soy sauce
1 tbsp mirin
1 tsp golden granulated sugar
1 tsp toasted sesame oil
1 tsp runny honey
½ tsp freshly cracked black pepper
150ml (5fl oz/scant ⅔ cup) mushroom soaking water or water

Soak the dried shiitake mushrooms in about 1 litre (34fl oz/4 cups) of cold water overnight in the fridge – they will plump up beautifully. Drain and reserve 150ml (5fl oz/scant ⅔ cup) of the soaking water (use the rest in soups and stocks).

Soak the *dangmyeon* in cold water for 20 minutes, then drain.

Put all the ingredients for the mushrooms in a mixing bowl, except the mushroom soaking water. Combine well and leave to marinate for 10 minutes.

Meanwhile, heat ½ tablespoon of vegetable oil in a large sauté pan over a medium heat. Sauté the onion with a pinch of salt for 2–3 minutes until the onion is softened but still with a little bite. Transfer to a large mixing bowl big enough to accommodate the rest of the ingredients. In the same pan, add another ½ tablespoon of oil and sauté the carrots with a pinch of salt for 2 minutes to soften. Tip the cooked carrots into the same bowl and add both chillies.

Heat 1 tablespoon of vegetable oil in the same pan over a medium heat. Add the mushrooms and sauté for 2 minutes. You should notice the smell of garlic and sweet soy sauce. Add the measured mushroom soaking water, let it bubble, then lower the heat to braise the mushrooms for 10 minutes, or until they have absorbed all the liquid. They should look glossy and plump. Check the seasoning and adjust it with a pinch more salt or sugar, if necessary. Remove from the heat to cool down a little before transferring to the bowl with the onion, carrots and chillies. Keep the pan aside for the time being, as we will come back to finish off the noodles in the pan.

Bring a large pan of water to boil. Add the noodles and stir in 1 tablespoon of vegetable oil. Cook the noodles according to the packet instructions until they are cooked through and appear more translucent. If you are unsure whether they are done, taste them. They should be springy and soft, but with a pleasantly chewy texture. Carefully drain the noodles and rinse with cold water a couple of times, then drain fully.

Roughly cut the noodles into manageable lengths with kitchen scissors and add to the mixing bowl with all the vegetables. Add the minced garlic, the sugar, soy sauce and sesame oil and seeds. Toss everything together to combine, preferably by hand. Transfer to the sauté pan you used earlier and warm the noodles over a medium heat, gently stirring (or tossing by hand, if you're like me) continuously. It should take 3–4 minutes. Transfer to a large platter and serve while warm.

Party Noodles

Janchi Guksu

Also known as banquet noodles, this warm and soothing bowl of noodles is a dish served on special occasions, often involving family gatherings – think weddings, birthdays and special celebrations. Adorned delicately with strips of crêpe-like omelette and tenderly seasoned vegetables, it looks perfectly elegant. It also graces the sticky tables of street-food stalls, although more rustic in its appearance, nourishing the souls of many hungry and tipsy customers.

The usual choice of broth for the dish is either beef or dried anchovy, depending on the region, with the main emphasis on giving the stock a depth of clean flavour known as *dambaekhan mat*. I am opting for a quick and easy method, relying on a few storecupboard ingredients to cheat my way into unlocking an umami flavour.

A quick soy sauce *dadaegi* on the side is an option that can help to further flavour the broth. Serve with small side plates of Turmeric Pickled Radish (page 110) and/or Fresh Kimchi (page 109) to add some crunchy texture to the meal.

SERVES 4

½ onion, sliced
two 5×7.5cm (2×3in) sheets of *dasima* (dried kelp)
2 tbsp *yondu* (seasoning sauce)
1 tbsp light or soup soy sauce
1 tbsp fish sauce
1.2 litres (40fl oz/4¾ cups) just-boiled water
sea salt flakes, to taste

For the toppings
2 eggs
sea salt flakes, to taste
2 tbsp vegetable oil
100g (3½oz) carrot, cut into 5cm (2in) batons, then julienned
200g (7oz) courgette (zucchini), sliced into thin half-moon shapes
1 garlic clove, grated
1 tbsp mirin

For the *dadaegi* sauce
3 tbsp soy sauce
1 tbsp toasted sesame oil
½ tsp golden granulated sugar
½ tsp *gochugaru* (Korean red pepper flakes)
¼ tsp ground white pepper
1 spring onion (scallion), thinly sliced
1 garlic clove, grated
1 hot green chilli, sliced

To serve
4 servings of *somyeon* or *somen* (thin dried wheat noodles)
some *gim jaban* (crumbled toasted seasoned seaweed), optional

Put the onion, *dasima*, *yondu*, light soy sauce, fish sauce and water into a heavy-based saucepan with a lid. Place it over a low heat and simmer gently with the lid on for 10 minutes until the flavours of the *dasima* are extracted and the onions are softened. Check for seasoning and adjust it with a pinch of salt, if necessary. When done, remove and discard the *dasima*. Keep the stock warm.

Make the *dadaegi* sauce by combining all the sauce ingredients in a small mixing bowl, then set aside.

Have a tray or plate ready to transfer the toppings as you go along.

Lightly whisk the eggs with about ¼ teaspoon of salt in a small mixing bowl. Heat ½ tablespoon of the vegetable oil in a non-stick frying pan (skillet) over a low heat and gently pour in the whisked eggs. Swirl the pan to spread out as thinly and evenly as possible. You will notice the top drying and the edge starting to set. Let it cook for a minute until the middle of the egg appears almost set, then carefully flip it over and cook for another 10 seconds on the other side. Transfer to a chopping board. Fold the sheet gently and slice into thin strips. Transfer to the tray and set aside.

Heat another ½ tablespoon of the vegetable oil in the same frying pan over a medium heat. Add the carrots and sauté gently for 2 minutes with a good pinch of salt until the carrots appear softened and smell fragrant. Remove from the heat. Transfer the carrots to the tray with the eggs. Set aside.

Give the same pan a quick wipe with kitchen paper, if necessary. Heat the remaining vegetable oil over a low heat. Add the courgettes and garlic and sauté gently for about 3 minutes with a good pinch of salt until the courgettes are softened. Stir in the mirin and cook for a further 2 minutes until the courgettes are tender. Transfer the courgettes to the tray with the eggs and carrots. Set aside.

Cook the noodles according to the packet instructions. Rinse with cold water to remove the starch and drain thoroughly. Divide the noodles and toppings among four bowls. Reheat the stock, if necessary, to ensure it is hot. Carefully pour the stock over the noodles and top with a sprinkle of *gim jaban* just before serving, if using. Serve with the *dadaegi* sauce on the side.

Stir-Fried Buttered Kimchi Udon

Kimchi Bokkeum Udong

I know there are already quite a few noodle recipes in this chapter that use kimchi as a main flavour building bock, but that is because kimchi is such a versatile ingredient that can really add impact to a dish with hardly any effort. Besides, Korean homes are never without kimchi in various stages of fermentation.

Over-ripe, sour-tasting kimchi is best suited to this dish; when softened in butter, its sharp, pungent edge mellows and as the cabbage cooks down, its floppy texture becomes more livened with a pleasant bite. The flavours of kimchi carried by lip-glossing fat are rich and luscious, kissing the bouncy noodles beautifully. Sprinkled greedily here are flakes of crunchy, salty-sweet seaweed that disappear into the depths of the tangy kimchi; the softness of the seaweed crumbs remain in the back palate, humming with notes of the gentle ocean.

It is a deliciously self-caring lunch for one, which can easily be multiplied for a larger crowd.

SERVES 1

1 serving of frozen
   udon noodles
20g (¾oz) unsalted butter
1 spring onion
   (scallion), sliced
1 garlic clove, minced
100g (3½oz) ripe cabbage
   kimchi, roughly chopped
½ tsp golden granulated
   sugar
¼ tsp freshly cracked
   black pepper
1 tsp mirin
1 tbsp soy sauce
1 tbsp perilla oil
sea salt flakes, to taste

To serve

1 soft-boiled egg, halved
2 tbsp *gim jaban*
   (crumbled toasted
   seasoned seaweed)
½ tsp toasted white sesame
   seeds, lightly crushed
a pinch of chilli powder
   (optional)

Soak the frozen udon noodles in just-boiled water for 1 minute to loosen. Drain and rinse in cold water before draining fully. Set aside. Now is a good time to boil the egg, too.

Melt the butter in a wok or sauté pan over a medium heat. Add the spring onion and garlic. Once the pan starts to sizzle and smells very fragrant, stir in the kimchi, sugar and black pepper. Lower the heat a touch and sauté for 5 minutes to soften the kimchi, stirring occasionally. Add the mirin and continue cooking for a further 1 minute until the kimchi is softened.

Increase the heat to high and swiftly stir in the udon noodles. Pour the soy sauce along the edge of the pan. Add the perilla oil and stir-fry for 2 minutes until everything is well combined and the noodles are cooked. Check for seasoning and adjust it with a pinch of salt, if necessary.

Remove from the heat and transfer to your favourite bowl. Top with the soft-boiled egg and *gim jaban*. Scatter with the crushed sesame seeds and a pinch of chilli powder, if using.

Street-Food Cart Udon

Pojangmacha Udong

For those who were born in the 1970s or 80s in Korea, this humble bowl of noodles will carry a certain kind of nostalgia, as it used to be served in most *pojangmacha* joints back in the day. It was always popular, not only because the soup pairs well with soju but also because the toothsome noodles and generous broth made a cheap and cheerful dinner that appealed to everyone.

Brothy noodles adorned with slivers of fried bean curd (*yubu*) and crumbled seaweed – the ocean-like sweet-saltiness permeates gently in the mouth as you slurp – delicately lifted by the refreshing bite of green spring onions. It's no wonder people used to describe the flavour of the broth as an honest taste.

Of course, you can take time building the backbone of the broth, layering it with depth of flavour using traditional Korean stock ingredients such as dried anchovies, *dasima* (dried kelp), dried mushrooms and the like, but I also think there are times that call for something far more straightforward and immediate. The version here is simple and speedy, utilizing a handful of well-considered storecupboard ingredients to satisfy the need for convenience and to deliver flavour.

SERVES 2

2 servings of frozen
    udon noodles
2 pieces of fried bean
    curd, cut into thin
    strips (optional)
sea salt flakes, to taste

For the broth
800ml (28fl oz/3½ cups)
    warm water, not boiling
one 5×7.5cm (2×3in) sheet
    of *dasima*
2 spring onions (scallions),
    white parts cut into
    batons, green parts
    thinly sliced to garnish
2 garlic cloves, crushed
2 tbsp light or soup
    soy sauce
2 tbsp mirin
1 tbsp *yondu* (seasoning
    sauce)
2 tsp Worcestershire sauce
¼ tsp ground white pepper

To finish
a small handful of peppery
    green leaves such
    as rocket (arugula),
    watercress or parsley
2 tbsp *gim jaban*
    (crumbled toasted
    seasoned seaweed)
a pinch of *gochugaru*
    (Korean red pepper
    flakes), optional

Put all the ingredients for the broth (except the green parts of the spring onions – we will use these later for the garnish) into a heavy-based saucepan with a lid that is large enough to accommodate the noodles. Bring just to the boil, then reduce the heat to simmer steadily for 15 minutes with the lid on ajar, until the vegetables are softened and their flavours extracted. Scoop out and discard the *dasima*, spring onions and garlic.

Stir in the udon noodles and fried bean curd strips, if using. Let it simmer for a couple of minutes, or until the noodles are cooked through according to the packet instructions. Check for seasoning and adjust it with a pinch of salt, if necessary.

Divide the noodles between two deep bowls. Top with the reserved green parts of the spring onions and a small handful of peppery green leaves of your choice. Finish the bowl with a sprinkle of *gim jaban* and a pinch of *gochugaru*, if using, just before serving.

Tomato + Kimchi Instant Noodle

Tomato Kimchi Ramyun

I don't know if there is a better impromptu slurp than instant noodles. It's cheap, it's fast and it's always on hand if you are like me, stashing away a couple of packs at the back of the cupboard for that emotionally ravenous moment that requires an immediate fix of familiar slurp.

While it may seem odd to write about how to cook packet noodles, I do feel that it does make sense to include a version of *ramyun* in here, as it is such an important part of Korean food culture. It's what most of us learn to cook first to satiate our hunger on a whim. We bond over the shared love of noodles slurped together late at night; a sure-fire way of initiating an intimate human connection. We all have our personal preference of how we like to cook the same packet of noodles and yet *ramyun*, to me, is an entirely universal dish that shouts COMFORT: a gateway to a Korean soul. And a version of mine goes something like this.

SERVES 1

1 tbsp vegetable oil
1 spring onion (scallion), white part sliced; the green part thinly sliced at an angle for garnish
1 garlic clove, minced
80g (3oz) ripe cabbage kimchi, roughly chopped
½ tsp golden granulated sugar
1 tomato, skinned and cut into 8 wedges
1 pack of Korean instant noodles (I like Shin or Ansungtangmyun)
480ml (16½fl oz/2 cups) just-boiled water
1 egg
parmesan, grated for garnish

Put the vegetable oil, the white part of the spring onion and the garlic in a cold, lidded saucepan (we will need the lid for poaching the egg). Place it over a medium heat to gently warm up the oil to infuse the flavours of the aromatics.

Once the pan starts to sizzle and smells very fragrant, stir in the kimchi and sugar. Lower the heat a touch and sauté for 5 minutes to soften the kimchi. Add the tomato and both the seasoning and dried vegetable sachets from the packet of noodles. Pour in the hot water and crank up the heat to bring to the boil. Add the noodles and cook on a medium–high heat for 2½ minutes (or for 3 minutes if you prefer more cooked noodles), stirring occasionally to loosen the noodles.

While the pan is still on a high heat, gently crack in the egg, then reduce the heat to low and put the lid on top to steam the egg for 1 minute; this will poach the egg with a runny yolk. Remove the pan from the heat but let it sit for another 30 seconds with the lid left on. Scatter with the reserved green part of the spring onion and grate over mounds of parmesan cheese. Slurp immediately – and carefully – while the noodles are bouncy and steaming hot.

Hangover Cure Soups

Koreans love to drink, which I think stems from the 'work hard and play hard' culture. Consequently, and not surprisingly, there is also a well-established culture of *haejangguk*: a group of soups enjoyed as a cure for a hangover, also known as *sulguk*. In the wee hours, a few market stalls open to serve market traders and late-night drinkers with hearty soups to soothe the stomach. The ingredients and seasoning vary depending on the regions and typically accommodate the seasonality and local palate.

Ugeoji, the outer leaves of cabbage or other greens, feature heavily, as do sundried cabbage leaves or radish tops called *siraegi*. And one of the most famous of this kind is a dish called *seonji haejangguk*, which includes congealed ox or pig's blood, though it is a real love-or-hate affair even among the locals.

The soups are not just for hangovers though. These delicious and comforting broths are fit for all occasions when we need a warmth to touch our delicate souls.

Hangover Cure Soup

Haejangguk

What we have here is a reasonably quick homestyle version of *haejangguk*. Using smaller chunks of beef and more widely available dark greens, the dish satisfies the need for something hearty with relative ease. While I have kept the process simple, I do remain respectful to the tradition by seasoning the blanched greens generously with a garlic-heavy paste before adding them to the soup – a cooking technique often used for many soups and stews – which helps to create a pleasing texture and wonderful, lingering depth of flavour.

SERVES 4

1 tbsp perilla oil
1 tbsp vegetable oil
3 spring onions (scallions),
    white parts and green
    parts separated, sliced
500g (1lb 2oz) beef shin,
    cut into 3cm (¼in) cubes
sea salt flakes, to taste
1.5 litres (56fl oz/
    6⅔ cups) water
two 5×7.5cm (2×3in) sheets
    of *dasima* (dried kelp)
250g (9oz) kale or
    turnip tops or cavolo
    nero, trimmed and
    roughly chopped

For the seasoning
7 garlic cloves, minced
2 tbsp light or soup soy sauce
2 tbsp mirin
1 tbsp *gochugaru* (Korean
    red pepper flakes)
1 tbsp perilla oil
1 tbsp *doenjang* (Korean
    fermented bean paste)
1 tbsp fish sauce

Preheat the oven to 160°C fan (180°C/350°F/gas 4).

Heat both the perilla and vegetable oils in a large, lidded, flameproof casserole dish. Add the white parts of the spring onions, the beef and a pinch of salt. Sauté gently for a few minutes over a medium heat, stirring frequently to coat the beef in the fragrant oil, for about 4 minutes until the beef has lightly browned. Add the water and *dasima* and bring to the boil, then remove from the heat.

Scrunch up a large sheet of parchment paper and make a drop lid by laying the paper right on top of the prepared dish to cover. Place the casserole lid on top and transfer to the oven. Leave to cook for 1½ hours.

Meanwhile, bring a pan of salted water to the boil. It would also be useful to have a bowl of cold water ready close by, so you can plunge the blanched kale immediately into the cold water. When the water is rapidly boiling, carefully drop in the kale and blanch for 1 minute until a little floppy. Lift out the wilted kale and transfer to a bowl of cold water, then drain. Gently squeeze the water out of the kale leaves by hand, without squashing them. Separate the leaves.

Make the sauce by combining all the sauce ingredients in a large mixing bowl. Add the blanched kale and toss well together, then set aside.

After 1½ hours, carefully remove the lid and the drop lid from the casserole dish. Stir in the kale mixture, before placing the drop lid and lid back on. Place the dish back in the oven and continue cooking for 1 hour until the beef and kale are tender.

Check for seasoning and adjust with a pinch more salt, if necessary. Divide the soup among deep bowls and top with the green parts of the spring onions. Serve while steaming hot with plain steamed rice.

Pork + Pearl Barley Soup

Dwaeji Bori Gukbap

The story goes that in the olden days, a warm bowl of soup was sold in inns to passing merchants and pedlars looking for a quick eat and cheap stay. Old kitchens with limited heat sources meant that while a vat of soup (often made with meat bones and/or vegetables) was kept warm for several hours, there was no way to reheat the already cooked – inevitably cold – rice. So the cooks started to pour the hot broth over the rice and drain it repeatedly as a way of moistening and reheating the rice, before finally filling the bowl with the soup. This ancient practice of heating and softening the rice with a ladleful of hot broth, known as *toryeom*, still continues in some traditional *gukbap* joints across Korea, as many cooks believe it primes the rice with the flavour of the broth to yield a more harmonious overall flavour.

Traditionally, the dish begins with a long and slow boil of meat and bones. Stirring a pot of brothy bean soup the other day, I realized *gukbap* bears a remarkable resemblance. Brothy pork and grains (or legumes) are the flavour combination adopted in many different ways across the continents, proven to offer a hug in a bowl: a good and proper soul food for all. It seems to make sense to me to adapt the method, relying on the sweetness of onions and leeks for convenience. As the hard grains of barley start to swell and soften, they release a milky white starch that thickens the broth. Finish the dish with a Korean flair of *dadaegi* sauce; a quick spicy seasoning sauce that further flavours an otherwise mild soup.

SERVES 6

185g (6½oz/1 cup) pearl barley
4 tbsp extra virgin olive oil
1½ onions, diced
250g (9oz) leek, halved lengthways and sliced 1cm (½in) thick
4 garlic cloves, minced
sea salt flakes, to taste
750g (1lb 10oz) pork shoulder or leg joint kept whole without skin
2 dried bay leaves
2.5 litres (85fl oz/10½ cups) just-boiled water

For the spicy *dadaegi* sauce

2 tbsp *gochugaru* (Korean red pepper flakes)
1 tbsp soy sauce
1 tbsp fish sauce
½ tsp ground white pepper
½ tsp golden granulated sugar

To serve

3 spring onions (scallions), thinly sliced
a knob of root ginger, as desired, julienned into thin matchsticks

Wash the pearl barley with cold water a few times to remove the starch until the water runs relatively clear, then soak the grains in cold water for 30 minutes to hydrate. Drain well and set aside.

Heat the olive oil in a heavy-based lidded saucepan and sauté the onions, leek and garlic with a generous pinch of salt, very gently over a low heat for 15 minutes, until the alliums are softened and cooked down sweet; it should smell deliciously fragrant. Add the pork and bay leaves. Give it a brief stir and top with the water, along with another generous pinch of salt. Bring just to the boil, then simmer gently over a low heat for 1 hour with the lid on.

Meanwhile to make the *dadaegi*, combine all the ingredients in a small bowl. Mix well and set aside.

After 1 hour, stir in the soaked and drained pearl barley. Simmer for a further 1 hour with the lid on until the grains are cooked plump and tender. Remove from the heat and leave to sit for 10 minutes. Lift out the pork and slice thinly.

Check the seasoning of the soup and adjust it with a pinch more salt, if necessary; although do bear in mind that if you're adding *dadaegi* to taste at the table, this is also salty. Divide into deep soup bowls, ensuring each bowl has enough grains, and top with the sliced meat. Scatter with the spring onions and ginger. Serve immediately while steaming hot with the *dadaegi* sauce on the side, to season the soup liberally right before eating.

Soybean Sprout Soup

Kongnamul Guk

Often found in larger Korean supermarkets, soybean sprouts are much nuttier and crunchier in taste and texture than the more common beansprouts (which are sprouted from mung beans), thanks to their more pronounced yellow heads and fibrous long stems. Commonly known for its hangover-relieving properties, this soup has a mild and deeply refreshing flavour and is much favoured by many as a breakfast dish to nurture a delicate appetite or chase away a sore head, while others simply appreciate the neutral flavour of the soup any time of the day.

The soup can be served both warm or chilled; fridge-cold soup can be cooled down even further with a few ice cubes – a much-welcomed remedy that livens up the wilting palate on a hot summer's day when the humid air clings to the skin, tight and sticky. It also pairs brilliantly with spicy dishes to offset the heat.

SERVES 4

300g (10½oz) soybean sprouts or beansprouts
two 5×7.5cm (2×3in) sheets of *dasima* (dried kelp)
2 tbsp fish sauce
1 tbsp *yondu* (seasoning sauce)
1.2 litres (40fl oz/4¾ cups) just-boiled water
2 garlic cloves, minced
2 spring onions (scallions), thinly sliced
2 hot green chillies (long finger or bird's eye), thinly sliced
½ tsp sea salt flakes

Prepare the soybean sprouts by removing any blackened heads and discoloured stems. It used to be said the wispy tail end of the stems should be trimmed, but nowadays it is believed that the more beneficial nutrients are found in those wispy ends. Plunge into a bowl of cold water to rinse and drain thoroughly. Set aside.

Put the *dasima*, fish sauce and *yondu* in a heavy-based, lidded saucepan and pour in half the amount of water. Bring to a gentle boil, then simmer for 5 minutes over a medium heat with the lid on. Add the soybean sprouts and garlic and simmer gently for 5 minutes until the soybean sprouts are cooked to your liking; I like to cook mine tender but with a bit of crunch left in them, but others prefer them completely soft – it's entirely up to you.

Remove and discard the *dasima*. Pour in the rest of the water and stir in the spring onion and chilli. Simmer very gently for a couple of minutes so that the flavours of spring onion and chilli can permeate the soup. Add the salt to season, then remove from the heat.

Serve with plain steamed rice or as an accompaniment to a spicy dish such as Oil Tteokbokki with Chilli Crisp + Honey (page 74), Spicy Stir-Fried Squid Deopbap (page 95) or Chuncheon-Style Spicy Stir-Fried Chicken (page 184).

If serving chilled, place the base of the saucepan in a bowl of cold water to cool as quickly as possible and then refrigerate – it should last for a couple of days. Serve with or without the addition of ice cubes.

Daikon Radish Soup

Mu Guk

I think a great pleasure is often to be found in simple dishes. Those reliable, tried-and-tested straightforward formulas that are ingrained in you like muscle memory that lets you glide and dance with ease through the kitchen to your own rhythm. It is those recipes that quietly sustain our weekly cooking repertoire and help us create fail-safe magic of the familiar taste we recall as comfort.

This radish soup to me, is one of those; a caring simmer of few ingredients harmoniously builds flavour to arrive at a soup that is deeply soothing. The gentle vegetal sweetness of radish comes forward and its unfussy flavours hug the palate. It is a delightfully clean-tasting bowl of soup and all the more joyous for its simplicity.

Eat with plain steamed rice or pour over some thin wheat or glass noodles if you want to make it a filling meal.

SERVES 4

400g (14oz) daikon radish, about 5mm (¼in) thick
2 tbsp perilla oil
2 garlic cloves, grated
½ tsp sea salt flakes
1 litre (34fl oz/4 cups) just-boiled water
two 5×7.5cm (2×3in) sheets of *dasima* (dried kelp)
1 tbsp *yondu* (seasoning sauce)
1 tbsp fish sauce
½ tsp ground white pepper
1 spring onion (scallion), thinly sliced

To julienne the radish, cut it into roughly 5cm (2in) long pieces first, then slice these thinly lengthways before cutting them into matchsticks.

Heat the perilla oil in a heavy-based saucepan with a lid over a medium heat. Add the radishes, garlic and salt, and sauté for 5 minutes, giving it a gentle stir from time to time. The radishes will change colour from opaque white to slightly translucent as they cook, and you should be able to smell the nutty aromas of the perilla oil as well as the faintly sweet scent of the radishes.

When the radishes have softened, add half the water and the *dasima*. Simmer gently over a low heat for 5 minutes with the lid on until the water has reduced slightly. Add the remaining water, along with the *yondu*, fish sauce and white pepper. Continue simmering for 5 minutes with the lid on until the radishes are tender. Remove and discard the *dasima*. Check for seasoning and adjust it with a pinch of salt, if necessary. Add the spring onion just before serving.

Pollock Soup

Bukeo Guk

The Korean language can be wonderfully descriptive and specific at times. I've learnt this is particularly true when it comes to pollock, which seems to have many different names depending on how the fish is processed. Pollock fish itself is called *myeongtae* but mostly goes by its other known name *saengtae* which describes a fresh and untreated pollock; *dongtae* for the frozen; *kodari* for the semi-dried; *bukeo* for the dried; *nogari* for the dried baby pollock. And then, there is *hwangtae*, which is pollock processed following a special drying technique that involves the removal of salt residue before hanging to air-dry in a cold winter climate; it repeats the process of being frozen and thawed over the course of two to four months to give the fish a unique chewiness and yellow colour.

Bukeo guk is one of two – the other being Soybean Sprout Soup (page 225) – quick and easy homestyle hangover cure soups, famously known for its effectiveness in detoxifying the liver and decomposing alcohol in the body. Strictly speaking, *bukeo* here describes a dried pollock. The dish is usually made by sautéing rehydrated (briefly soaked in water) dried pollock strips in a toasted sesame oil to build the savoury backbone; the soup is then silkened and bulked out with eggs for sustenance.

I am using fresh pollock for this recipe as it is more widely available, so the dish technically isn't exactly the same, but I find the soothing flavour is very similar.

SERVES 4

270g (10oz) pollock fillets
sea salt flakes
1 tbsp toasted sesame oil
¼ onion, thinly sliced
2 spring onions (scallions),
  sliced; green parts
  reserved for garnish
2 garlic cloves, minced
two 5×7.5cm (2×3in) sheets
  of *dasima* (dried kelp)
1 litre (34fl oz/4 cups)
  just-boiled water
1 tbsp mirin
1 tbsp fish sauce
1 tbsp *yondu* (seasoning
  sauce)
¼ tsp ground white pepper
1–2 hot green chillies,
  thinly sliced

For the eggs

3 eggs
1 tbsp mirin
1 tsp rice vinegar
½ tsp sea salt flakes

Pat the fish dry with kitchen paper and lay it on a flat tray in one single layer. Sprinkle evenly with about ½ teaspoon of salt; this will help the flesh of the fish to firm up, giving a slightly drier bite when cooked in the soup. Refrigerate, uncovered, while you get on with the rest of the prep.

Heat the sesame oil in a heavy-based saucepan with a lid and sauté the onion and the white parts of the spring onions with a good pinch of salt over a low heat for 5 minutes until the onions are softened. Add the garlic, give it a brief stir and cook for 1 minute; it should smell very fragrant. Add the *dasima* and water. Simmer gently over a low heat for 20 minutes with the lid on ajar.

Meanwhile, crack the eggs into a bowl or a small jug with a pouring spout. Season with the mirin, vinegar and salt, and whisk to combine. Set aside.

After 20 minutes, you should notice the wonderfully fragrant smell of the stock. Scoop out and discard the *dasima*. Increase the heat to medium and season with the mirin, fish sauce, *yondu* and white pepper. Add the pollock fillets and simmer steadily for 4 minutes, with the lid on ajar, until the fish is cooked through and flaking. Check for seasoning and adjust with a pinch more salt, if necessary. You may want to break up the fish a little to make bite-sized pieces.

Keep the pan on a high simmer, just below boiling. Hold the whisked eggs in your dominant hand, close to the pan and steadily pour in the egg in circular motion. Don't touch the pan too much once the egg is in. Let the pan come back up to a high simmer. When you see the egg floating back up to the surface, stir in the chilli and reserved green parts of the spring onions. Remove from the heat and stand for 2 minutes with the lid on to gently infuse the flavours of the chilli and spring onions in a residual heat.

Ladle the soup among four deep bowls and serve immediately with plain steamed rice.

NIGHTCAP

An old saying goes that soju tastes sweet or bitter depending on your mood. Here I gathered a small selection of soju-based cocktails to warmly welcome you into the night. The recipes are straightforward but, as a general rule, soju is best kept cold in the fridge, and make sure to use the best-quality ice for your cocktails straight from the freezer. The measurement 'a dash' is about 10 drops of liquid. Have fun making them and enjoy responsibly!

Soju on the Rocks

MAKES 1

ice cubes
50ml (1 measure)
  premium-quality soju
a twist of lemon peel,
  to garnish

Soju is most often enjoyed cold in a shot glass, either sipped or downed in one. However, more flavourful premium versions can be so much more pleasurable when sipped slowly, poured over a few cubes of ice. You can, of course, use a standard bottle of soju, though for this recipe, I really recommend sourcing a premium quality with around 25 per cent alcohol.

Fill a large, heavy tumbler with ice cubes and pour the soju over. Stir continuously to chill the soju. Garnish with a twist of lemon peel with oil from the peel briefly rubbed around the rim of the glass.

Soju + Tonic with a Twist

MAKES 1

ice cubes
100ml (2 measures) soju
150ml (3 measures) tonic
a dash of Angostura bitters
a wedge or cheek of lime,
  to garnish

A twist on classic gin and tonic, it's floral on the nose with a peachy sophistication. *Pictured on page 236.*

Fill a tall glass with ice cubes and pour the soju over. Stir continuously to chill the drink down. Top with the tonic and add the Angostura bitters. Squeeze the lime over the drink before garnishing.

Old Seoul

MAKES 1

ice cubes
100ml (2 measures) soju
1 tbsp syrup from a jar
  of cocktail cherries
  (I used Opies brand
  for this recipe)
a dash of orange bitters
a cocktail cherry from
  the jar, to garnish
a twist of orange peel,
  to garnish

A nod to a classic Old Fashioned, this is a longer cocktail of almost neat soju. *Pictured on page 237.*

Fill a large heavy tumbler with ice cubes and pour the soju over. Stir continuously to chill the soju down. Stir in the syrup and orange bitters. Garnish with a cherry and the orange peel.

Soju Sour

MAKES 1

ice cubes
50ml (½ measure) soju
25ml (½ measure)
  lemon juice
12ml (¼ measure)
  maple syrup
1 tsp syrup from a jar
  of Maraschino cherries,
  plus 1 cherry, to garnish
  (I like Luxardo brand
  for this recipe)
a slice of lemon, to garnish

Classic sour cocktails are known for their sherbet-like sharpness
balanced against the sweet. This is deliciously zingy.

Fill a large cocktail shaker with ice cubes and add the soju, lemon juice and
maple syrup. Shake well to combine, then strain over a glass filled with ice.
Drizzle in the Maraschino cherry syrup and garnish with the cherry and slice
of lemon.

Seoul Mule

MAKES 1

crushed ice
100ml (2 measures) soju
25ml (½ measure) lime juice
150ml (3 measures) non-
  alcoholic ginger beer
a twist of lime peel

While I am usually more of a short and strong kind of cocktail person,
I do like the refreshing quality of classic mule variations that offer
satisfying relief when the summer heat is at its fiercest. Use a good-
quality spicy ginger beer to add a bit of kick! *Pictured on page 240.*

Fill a tall glass with crushed ice. Pour the soju over and stir to combine.
Add the lime juice and top with the ginger beer. Garnish with the lime peel.

Soju Spritz

MAKES 1

ice cubes
50ml (1 measure) soju
25ml (½ measure) sweet
  red vermouth
about 150ml (3 measures)
  Prosecco
a twist of orange peel

Anything topped with fizz is a good drink in my book. The red
vermouth adds a touch of sweetness and a sundowner-worthy
pale golden-orange hue. *Pictured on page 241.*

Fill a stemmed glass with ice cubes. Sir in the soju and vermouth and top
up with Prosecco. Garnish with the orange peel.

Index

Thank You

In the midst of writing this book about my hometown – a place that never fails to deliver deliciousness lit with neon-rainbow lights and seasoned with a dose of humour and generosity – my father, encouraged by my mother, left his home in Seoul for good to start a quieter, new life. He is a born-and-bred city boy whose grit and soul are dedicated to the city. He grew taller alongside the city's ever-expanding landscapes and skyscrapers. The move – an act of leaving his story behind – made him depressed and his appetite for life started to fail. In January 2023, he fell very ill and was in a coma for 12 long days, his physical body deteriorating rapidly, until he woke up again dreaming of iced coffee in Seoul, his (late) parents and his grandchildren near and far.

My father is the most loving man, but I'd failed to express my love to him as a child growing up. He has since made a full recovery, but the experience has made me forever more aware of the fragility of our hearts and the search for a sense of home. I am grateful for his strength. This book would not be here if it wasn't for my father's mischievous and charming ways, which showed me the electric magic of what Seoul had to offer growing up. And I cannot thank him enough. 아빠, 사랑해: Daddy, I love you.

My heartfelt gratitude for each one of you – readers, reviewers, cooks and booksellers – who have supported my writing journey by giving my first book, *Rice Table*, a good home. It has been one of the greatest privileges seeing the well-worn pages of my book splattered with *gochugaru* stains and covered in notes and marked with tabs. It is because of your love and support that I get to continue writing. This book would not be here without your readership, so thank you.

I have learned that creating a book – especially a cookbook – is truly collaborative work involving much expertise. I feel incredibly lucky to have been able to join forces again with such a talented group of people I sincerely admire. It is with their labour of love and honest effort that we're able to transform an idea in my head into a beautiful object we can physically touch. I am very grateful for my dream team and I would like to hold onto them dearly.

Sarah Lavelle, and everyone behind the scenes at Quadrille, thank you so much for giving me another opportunity to write.

Emily, I still pinch myself that I get to do what I love doing the most. Your honest advice and gentle ways are always deeply appreciated.

Harriet, you are the most compassionate and loving editor. Thank you for giving me the creative freedom to write. It is with your trust that I get to grow as a writer and be the person I have always dreamed of becoming.

Lucy, thanks so much for being so open and accepting of my wildest ideas, and materializing them in the most evocative ways; the book is every inch stunning.

Rachel, thank you so much for taking me on a journey, revealing a different kind of calm and elegance, this time in full colour. The props and the way you visualized them to tell the story of pocha have made for beautiful and mouthwateringly delicious photos.

Tamara, my incredibly talented super woman, I am simply in awe of the beautiful mess you can create with my humble recipes. Thank you so much for all the magic you inject onto the plates.

Emma, Sophie and El, thank you all for your support. Please do know that it never goes unnoticed – without your help, we wouldn't have been able to run such tightly scheduled days so smoothly.

Ben, our dearest friend, thanks so much for being there for Toby and me. Your quiet brilliance is weaved in every single image we shot together, and I am very grateful that you have chosen to invest your time in this book.

Wendy, I learn so much from the process back and forth with you. Thank you for your vigilant ways that help me notice the small details.

Joyce and Chris, thanks so much for keeping my head in a good place and for lending me your gorgeous glassware; the Soju Sour on page 238 is for you.

My amazing mother-in-law, Hazel, thank you for taking care of Kiki whenever we needed help. I read somewhere that the happiness of a woman's career is dependant on the quality of childcare available – I am a very happy writer.

Lastly, two of my favourite people. Toby, thank you for translating my words into something beautiful to look at. But, more importantly, I'd like to thank you for carrying the weight of our life while holding me tight when I needed it the most. And my darling Kiki, thanks for walking twenty-odd-thousands steps with me in Seoul everyday and for helping me visualize the story of my heart. Pocha is your book as much as it is mine. I am so grateful for our family bond that helps us grow and better ourselves every day. Team Scott, we did the bestest! X

Managing Director: Sarah Lavelle
Commissioning + Project Editor: Harriet Webster
Copy Editor: Wendy Hobson
Designer + Illustrator: Studio Polka
Photographer: Toby Scott
Photography Assistant: Benjamin Wisely
Food Stylist: Tamara Vos
Prop Stylist: Rachel Vere
Head of Production: Stephen Lang
Senior Production Controller: Sabeena Atchia

First published in 2024 by Quadrille, an imprint of Hardie Grant Publishing

Quadrille
52–54 Southwark Street
London SE1 1UN
quadrille.com

ISBN: 978 1 83783 116 6
Printed in China